PRODUCER
TO
PRODUCER

The Best of Michael Wiese in *VIDEOGRAPHY* Magazine

by Michael Wiese

Edited by Brian McKernan
Editor, VIDEOGRAPHY

Published by Michael Wiese Productions, 4354 Laurel Canyon Blvd., Suite 234, Studio City, California 91604, (818) 379-8799.

Cover Design by Charles Field, Fieldworks, Los Angeles
Author Photograph and Indonesian photographs by Geraldine Overton

Printed by Braun-Brumfield, Inc., Ann Arbor, Michigan
Manufactured in the United States of America

Note: The information presented in this book is for educational purposes only. The author is not giving business or financial advice. Readers should consult their lawyers and financial advisors on their business plans and procedures. The publisher is not liable for how readers may choose to use this information.

The publisher plants two trees for every tree used in the manufacturing of this book. Printed on recycled stock.

Library of Congress Cataloging–in–Publication Data

Wiese, Michael, 1947–
   Producer to producer: the best of Michael Wiese in Videography magazine/
   by Michael Wiese; edited by Brian McKernan
        p.   cm.
     ISBN 0-941188-15-9
     1. Video recordings--Production and direction. 2. Television- Production and direction. I. McKernan, Brian. II. Title.
PN1992.94.W49   1993
791.43'0973--dc20   93-23177
                                                                  CIP

Books by MICHAEL WIESE

Producer to Producer
Film & Video Financing
Film & Video Marketing
Home Video: Producing for the Home Market
Film & Video Budgets
The Independent Film & Videomakers Guide

Audiotapes by MICHAEL WIESE

The American Film Institute Seminar: Financing & Marketing Video

Books from MICHAEL WIESE PRODUCTIONS

Film Directing: Shot by Shot by Steven D. Katz
Film Directing: Cinematic Motion by Steven D. Katz
Fade In: The Screenwriting Process by Robert A. Berman
The Writer's Journey: Mythic Structure for Storytellers & Screenwriters by Christoper Vogler

FOR

B. B. WIESE, my father, a man of integrity,
GERALDINE OVERTON-WIESE, my loving wife,
JULIA BRONWYN, our new daughter, already an explorer

TABLE OF CONTENTS

ACKNOWLEDGMENTS

A lot of people can make one person look really good.

I am very grateful to Brian McKernan, friend and editor of *Videography* magazine. When I mentioned the idea of compiling these articles into a book, he enthusiastically came to the rescue with his fully-edited floppy disks of the articles. (Unless you've read my raw manuscripts, you don't have any idea how valuable an editor's input is!) *Videography* publisher Paul Gallo also supported the project from the get-go. I can't tell you how delightful it is to "get it done" when you are supported by people as terrific as the folks at *Videography*.

Rick Stromoski is a new acquaintance of mine, but is not new to his fans who are readers of many national magazines in which his work appears frequently. His wonderful illustrations give us a chance to laugh at ourselves in those all too frequent, high-pressured moments common to the video business.

Graphic designer Charles Field has created a fabulous cover that makes you look twice.

My thanks go to Robin Quinn who brought her meticulousness to proofread and correct the final pages. (How does anybody have that much patience?)

I am grateful to MWP account manager Ken Lee who managed the book production process by overseeing all the elements, making sure they got to the right place at the right time, and for reading, then re-reading everything herein even though he hears it on a daily basis. What fortitude! What stamina! What dedication!

My wife Geraldine Overton is the smart one in our family. She was the one that suggested I compile all these articles into a book. She probably came up with the idea after remembering the early morning/late night writing that went into the last book *(Film and Video Financing)*, and thought this would be a quick and easy book. (It was.) It's also her photograph of the author on the back cover.

And lastly, my thanks go to the readers of *Videography* Magazine who have written and called over the years, asked their questions, participated in consulting sessions, and contributed their own knowledge and experience to my memory banks.

Without all of you, there would be no books, and no one with whom to share this information. I hope you find it useful.

Michael Wiese
Studio City, CA
May 19, 1993

FOREWORD
by Brian McKernan

I first met Michael Wiese in 1990 at a UCLA Extension seminar on the then-new topic of "desktop video." Michael had organized the event, which turned out to be one of the most useful I'd ever attended. Lecturers included people I've come to regard as visionaries on the uses and impacts of media's digital future: Eric Martin, Dean of the California Institute of the Arts; Michael Nesmith, President of Pacific Arts and creator of the first "music video"; and Scott Billups, producer/director extraordinaire and one of America's leading media integrators.

By the end of the day, the opportunities of the new visual media were foremost on everyone's mind. Martin likened technology's quickening evolution to a giant vortex. Nesmith observed that virtual reality was a window into a new world that requires us to expand our communication abilities. And Billups showed a tape of his desktop facility that prompted executives from video and computer companies to sequester him in a back room for an ad hoc mind meld.

Michael had organized and moderated a knockout seminar, but–interestingly enough–in my subsequent conversations with him he emphasized the enduring importance of the business side of production. If you can't sell what you've produced, he argued, you're not producing. The new economies of media technology are opening wide the gates of production opportunity; an entire new universe of video professionals needs to learn the basics of how to find the capital to fund their dreams. This was a subject Michael knew intimately, having launched more than 200 programs that cumulatively grossed over $60 million at companies such as Vestron Video.

Continuing our dialogue, Michael and I came to the mutual agreement that he be designated a *Videography* magazine Contributing Editor with his own column, *Producer to Producer. Videography* became the monthly magazine of professional video technology, production and applications in 1976, when portable cameras and VTRs ushered in a new era of visual communication. Fourteen years later, with the emergence of Video Toasters, CD ROM and digital studios, *Videography* continued its leadership as the information resource for video professionals at all levels. Michael's column, meanwhile, would ensure that readers would be exposed to innovative business ideas as part of our editorial package.

This book is a collection of Michael's *Producer to Producer* columns, which I've had the honor to edit at *Videography*. They await your attention, so–as Michael would say–now go get 'em!

Brian McKernan
Editor, *Videography*
New York

INTRODUCTION

INTRODUCTION

Writing the *Producer to Producer* columns for *Videography* magazine has been very rewarding. It's given me a timely outlet for up-to-the-minute knowledge recently harvested from my own fields of endeavor from location shooting to infomercials, from money-raising to marketing.

My process has always been to work hard, learn a lot, and then share the most relevant information with colleagues and fellow film- and videomakers. I am very passionate and committed to this sharing aspect. It is part of my contribution. It's painfully clear how important and valuable the right information is; without it, we would all have perished at the hands of clients, distributors or co-production partners. Learning first-hand is time-consuming and expensive. Learning from others speeds up your time on the learning curve and saves money.

In rereading the articles, I was pleased to see that they evenly covered the entire creative spectrum from program development, financing, production, through marketing and distribution. For the most part, I found the information as timely and valuable as when I first wrote it. At the beginning of most articles, I've added a little nugget to bring a reflective spirit or new perspective to the article.

There's nothing we can't accomplish. We just need the right information at the right time. I hope that the ideas in this book will bring you success in your own projects.

DEVELOPMENT

CONSULTING SESSION I

Consultants have an edge. They aren't "in the soup" and are able to see things clearly. To jar your own sensibilities and to help return your own clarity, listen without judgment to people outside your projects for every "whack-a-doo" idea. You'll be surprised what you might learn.

I'm a producer. I'm also a distributor/marketer. This gives me an edge, and so I have lots of consulting clients.

After leaving Vestron, I started a consulting business which parallels my production and publishing businesses. It all fits together and makes sense, although to outsiders it doesn't always look that way. Producers buy my books, and if they want further information they can call me. Some become consulting clients. Although most have some pieces of the video marketing puzzle figured out, they look to me to help direct them to the other pieces–design production, budgets, and distribution strategies that will get their programs made and distributed.

Sometimes I will produce their programs. Although my three businesses appear very different, they do fit together. I've been able to cross-market my services as a publisher, consultant, producer and marketer.

My consulting clients have problems. And most of them have the same problems. Since they are video producers, I assume that many of you have these problems as well. So save some bucks, and read on.

Consultants have the ability to look at a client's problems, see them afresh, and offer solutions in what looks like breakthroughs. Part of the reason for this is that a consultant's special knowledge can speed up the process for his client in reaching a goal. The client has been in a thick "pea soup" for so long, struggling with the problem, that he or she can no longer think clearly about it. Enter the consultant.

What follows are common problems of many producers. See anyone you know?

1. You Don't Have an Audience in Mind.

Producers rarely think about the audience who will watch or buy their program. They are too concerned with budgets, schedules, casting and political maneuvers to pay attention to one of the most important aspects of production on which the very real success of their program hinges.

Solution: Ask yourself specifically who makes up your market. Write it down. Where do they live? What is their income? Look at their level of education, sex and other psycho-demographics. What does your program have to offer your audience? Make sure it delivers to your audience. And how are you going to let them know about your program?

2. You Don't Know Whether or Not Distribution Channels Exist.

Even if they can identify their audience, a producer may not be sure of this.

Solution: Do your homework and research these issues before you roll any tape. Is there a television series that may acquire your single show? Does your program meet the criteria of that series? Is there a home video or non-theatrical or industrial distributor that can (and will want to) distribute your program? Is your program the correct length?

3. You Don't Know Where to Look for Markets.

Producers are very adept at solving production problems, but downright lazy when it comes to finding distribution information.

Solution: There are numerous books (including my own) and reference works that list film and video distributors. But that's not enough. You must start calling around and find those that specialize in your kind of product. If you ask the right questions, by the third phone call you should be hot on the trail of the handful of distributors appropriate for your product.

4. You Over-produced for the Marketplace.

Producers like to produce. And they'll spend whatever money they can get their hands on, even if it's not appropriate. I know of a producer who spent $500,000 on a sports video and was only able to recoup a $30,000 advance from the distributor. But he didn't care. He worked with two big sports stars, shot for days, ran up a hefty expense account, bought expensive music, and has a great "portfolio piece." Most of these things were inappropriate to the level of sales that the video would most likely have. He should have spent about $75,000. Pity the investors.

Solution: Have realistic expectations about what your video or television program can actually earn once it's in distribution. Most producers like to fool themselves (and their investors) and think more about producing the world's greatest video. Sometimes the market doesn't need the world's greatest video.

5.   You Under-Produced for the Market.

The converse of the above is also true. I recently saw a program that was produced for less than $30,000. It was intended for the business market. The producer was expecting to sell his one-hour tape for $500. The tape was underproduced for the market. The business and industry market is very sophisticated. They want valuable information. They are accustomed to commercial television standards.

Solution: The producer should have studied the market (he didn't) to check the quality, production and information levels of the programs being offered at $500 each. He would have spent 5-10 times his actual budget to increase the production value of his program and quadrupled the information he was presenting. He also could have produced a printed workbook or reference book, and put it all in an exquisite package.

6.   You Have Special Knowledge, But Don't Know How to Apply It to the Product.

This is probably part of being too deep in the "pea soup." A producer does not see his or her own expertise. Often a producer or creator of a program idea has special knowledge of the subject area as well as the marketplace and doesn't know it.

Solution: Perhaps you need a consultant to bring out those characteristics and help package it successfully. It's hard to see your own aces sometimes.

7.   You Refuse To Co-Venture.

Producers are control freaks. By gosh, they are going to do their own thing by themselves no matter what. I guess that's all right, but it takes longer and expends all their resources. If the program goes belly up in the marketplace (or never reaches the marketplace), they have only themselves to blame.

Solution: The world is full of support. Money, ideas, resources, sweat equity. You just have to ask. Sometimes the research it takes to find the co-venture partners is well spent. You may have to look in other walks of life and to people with entirely different life experiences than your own. They will have contacts and resources that you cannot access on your own. Spread the risks; share the wealth.

8.   You Have Produced a Great Program, But Don't Know What to do With It.

This is perhaps the most heartbreaking thing to see. People come to me with their half-baked, poorly executed programs that they've spent five years producing. It is immediately clear that their program doesn't have a snowball's chance.... It's not enough to tell them that their photography looks good or you really liked the way they did their titles. Sometimes the truth hurts, but it can keep them from making the same bad mistakes over the next five years.

Solution: None. Why? Because usually they did not have an audience in mind. Therefore their program has no marketing elements that will entice a distributor, let alone an audience, in their program. That's usually the case. (At Vestron, my original program division received 3000 unsolicited submissions: scripts, footage and finished programs. We bought three! And these, we twisted and turned and added in other elements before they were completed. The people who submitted ideas and furnished videos (quite a few were accomplished producers) didn't know the market. Period.

These are just some of the problems my clients bring me. I've seen them before, and I'll see them again. But not from you, right? Hopefully, this will give you some food for thought. Now until next time, go get 'em.

CONSULTING SESSION II

Last month I wrote about the common problems that many of my video producer clients bring me. Well, here I am again, with the balance of the 13 most common producer problems (and solutions). I hope these examples help you to swim to the top of your own "bowl of pea soup" (the confusing mix of questions and knowledge gaps plaguing producers trying to market their products), and to clearly see what must be done to achieve the success you seek.

9. You Don't Know How to Find or Match Sponsors to Their Programs.

This is a tough problem. Producers are looking to sponsors to finance and/or market their programs. Every other day some client says to me, "This would be terrific for Pepsi (or Honda, IBM, etc.) to sponsor!" That's really easy to say, but too often the producer is looking at the sponsorship match entirely from his or her own point of view.

Why would a sponsor want to finance or market or cross promote your program? Are the demographics the same for their product? How do you know that? How do you know they aren't working on opening up new demographics that you don't know about? Furthermore, corporations are working on promotions and marketing plans two years out. Sure, once in a while, there's some discretionary funds, and someone just happens to walk in at the right time and <u>whammo</u>! it happens. But that's very unusual.

I've been a part of a dozen or so sponsorship deals, and I can tell you that it's pure serendipity that brings sponsors and programs together. What producers will never know is the sponsor's agenda. There's no way to find out exactly what they want. Not even their ad agencies are sure from one moment to the next what will please the sponsor.

Solution: You can send out dozens, heck, hundreds of proposals. But it's generally a waste of postage and photocopying. Besides, the development departments of the dozen or so producing PBS stations are already going after anyone you'll ever target. And these folks are professionals armed with some of the best packaged ideas from America's top producers. But don't let that stop you.

What might be a better approach is to produce your program, and then send it to potential sponsors who might use it as a "premium." Once it's finished, a sponsor can see it. Be sure <u>not to include</u> a given brand-name product in your program. If that company nixes it, you'll never be able to go to their competition. If they like it, you can sell 50,000 or 100,000 videos to them to use in their promotions, and maybe sell more videos to a non-competing sponsor. Try to pull together your video without a sponsor. If you can leverage a major star, then sponsorship becomes more interesting. There's not enough space here to go into everything you can do, but know that sponsorship is great when it happens, very hard to get, and takes a long time to acquire.

10. You Don't Understand Distribution Deals.

By the time a producer gets to a distributor's doorstep, he or she is probably broke, very tired, and may even be sick of their own project. They want a vacation, and certainly need a deal to put their project to bed. This is not a good posture for negotiation. But it happens all the time. Every week I meet someone like this. They are ready to just turn their program over to a distributor, as they are so happy to have found anyone. They'd like to turn and walk away from the distribution problem. This is not the time to let your defenses down.

Solution: Producers should study distribution. They should read magazine articles on it (such as my columns in *Videography*), read books (you know whose), and talk to all their producer friends. If a distributor makes you an offer, get their catalog and call several of the producers whose product is handled by that distributor. Ask them their experience. Go through the details of their deals. There is no such thing as a "standard distribution" agreement. What you get is what you (and your lawyer) are able to negotiate.

11. You Don't Know How to Design a Marketing Plan.

Producers often don't know what they need. They don't know what marketing is. They want their programs to sell, but don't know that marketing is as important and sometimes more important than the actual content of their programs.

Solution: I'm frequently asked to help producers design their marketing plan and materials. This is a very complex task, but follows a logical course. The notion is to use whatever tools necessary to get to their audience. This could involve the design of a cassette package, a sell sheet, counter displays, advertisements, direct mail pieces, press releases, publicity and promotional tours. The marketing takes the form of a plan–a campaign over time–where different media (television, radio, print) may well be used to sell their videos. Sometimes the sales promotion will coincide with a television broadcast of their program or with the release of a book that has the same name. How do producers know what they need? That's a tough one. Producers could study similar programs or videos and examine the marketing strategies they used.

12.   You Did Things Out of Order, Then Got Stuck.

This is fairly common. Producers do things back-asswards. This takes a myriad of forms, but they forget the key task in producing.

Solution: A producer's job is to amass enough agreement (which is expressed as "someone else's money") to get the project off the ground. Producers should put together elements which will attract the other elements. For example, once you've got your script, money, producer, director and broadcaster then you can go after a star.

13.   You're Thinking of Standalone Programs, Not a Series or Line.

For all the talent that resides in a producer's brain, there are often gaps. I've met many producers who've worked for years to write and develop their one short video or one single hour program. That's fine; it really is. However, they frequently miss a terrific opportunity.

Solution: First, if you or your writers are experts in a subject area, it behooves you to think of a dozen program ideas before settling on one. In doing so, you may discover that you have a television series or a series of television programs in front of you. It is not necessarily any harder to raise the money for a series. And it is certainly easier to find a distributor or syndicator for a series than it is for a "one-off." (If you've ever made a single-hour program and tried to sell it to television you know what I mean.)

Okay, you say. You like the idea, but you want to start with one show and see how it does. Fine. Test out the market with your one video program. If it works, then branch out within the subject area. Remember, it's more expensive to market one video than a series of videos. If you and your distributor open up a market with one program, you should continue to work that market with follow-up programs. Don't think single programs, think <u>lines</u>.

When I published my first book, I made sure that the cover design was such that subsequent books could have a similar design. That's line thinking. The marketplace is now used to seeing the books and looks for more. In consulting with large program producers like *National Geographic, Nova, Smithsonian,* and *PBS* as well as smaller program producers of diving, surfing, music, how-to and health videos, I've recommended that they all develop lines of programming. There's no reason why you can't do the same thing. Five years from now you could have a line, a corner on a market, and a developed image of as a video publisher within that marketplace.

Does that answer all your questions? Feel better? Good for you. I'm beat. Now go get 'em!

13

FREE $1000 CONSULTING SESSION

Everyone falls into ruts in their thinking. I continually try to trick myself into new awareness. The more ways I can sneak up on an idea, the more likely I am to find new value. One thing I like to do is free associate. I take an idea and then brainstorm around it–listing everything that comes to mind. Sometimes combinations of elements lead to a third element that is really fresh.

There's nothing like a good headline to get your attention. Offer to give something away, and the masses will flock to you.

Now that I've piqued your interest, let me ask you a few questions. Do you want to increase revenue flow from your productions? Do you want to increase, and even expand, your audience? Do you want to take all that hard work you've put into developing and producing your video and build a business around it? If so, this column is for you. You'll learn just how important these ideas are when you start applying them as you develop your next projects.

Thinking Big

In our consulting business, the notion of "thinking big" surfaces daily. It doesn't matter if the client is a large broadcaster, home video company, or a small producer. It doesn't matter whether the issue is product development, production, marketing or distribution. "Thinking big" is usually a matter of solutions. Turning an idea into an operating principle in your own work is worth far more than the $1000 you didn't pay for this consulting session. Hey, you are getting something for free!

What You Already Know

By the time you've completed your production, you've spent weeks, months or even years developing your concept, doing research, writing treatments, scripts, final scripts and narration. You may have created storyboards, original art work, graphics, photographs, videotape, and soundtracks. You've structured your material first on paper and then executed a version on video. The finished piece has then made its way through some distribution process–large or small. There has probably been some audience reaction (through a purchase, an evaluation or review, or television ratings). Every producer has done an enormous amount of concentrated work. And the result is usually only one program.

So what's wrong with that? Perhaps nothing. But maybe you've missed opportunities that would expand your original idea into other products, sending your message far and wide.

Let's back up. Say you're ready to produce a half-hour training video, a home video, or a television program. It could be for in-house corporate distribution or consumer distribution. In either case, what normally happens is in the very first development meeting the die is cast–everyone starts talking about one product based on one idea. Why not, however, look at that one idea and slowly turn it to examine its every facet? Why not see what other communication pieces can be developed and produced?

Take out a piece of paper, and brainstorm. Anything goes. And at this stage, it costs you nothing.

Imagine the Possibilities

Here's a list of some products, or as I like to call them, "communication pieces," because they all present the original concept in different forms. Look them over. Ask yourself the following question, substituting each product listed in the second blank space provided. It's great fun and often productive. Give it a try.

"_____ is my concept. Can it be a _____?"

Product choices: feature film; videocassette; television program; television series; educational video; training video; video series; audio series; CD; CD-I; computer program; board game; text book; paperback book; synopsis; storyboard; illustrated book; book; workbook; planbook; photo book; poster; postcard; comic strip; press release; radio interview; television interview; seminar; appliance; invention; doll; action figure; lunch pail; pajamas; model; clothing line; food; franchise trademark.

Once you start working with this sentence and get the hang of it, you can easily add many more products to this list. One product will suggest several other forms.

Now, I am not suggesting that your every concept will father (or mother) every product listed above as one of its offspring. But this process frees your mind to see beyond the original form you invisioned for your idea.

Look at it this way. You have a concept. Is it worthy of expression in other forms? If so, what are those forms? Even if it is worthy of only a few forms, you've doubled or tripled your ability to communicate and generate awareness and revenues.

With all the upfront research you have to do and with all the writing inherent in most projects, why not think bigger and see if you can develop a line of programs and/or products? If it takes you a year to create your program, why not spend a year or two and create an entire product line around the same theme or concept? It will not cost you one cent more to think this way. If there are other opportunities, then you can work up business and marketing plans that will exploit the products you've created.

Here are some real-life examples.

From Documentary to Franchise

I recently reviewed a project that was initially designed as a series of historical documentaries. The research revealed some remarkable discoveries that have changed society's view of history. To illustrate this new point of view, 3-D computer models would be necessary. At this stage, the concept was so compelling that a major movie star agreed to host the program—making a network series possible. Because the producers started to think about what elements they needed for the documentary, they began to discover that other communication pieces or products could be created. They saw how their vast research generated a series, led to visualizing that research, excited a major star, and made a network series possible. The network series allowed international television and home video to be feasible.

From the vast research done for this project, they could create books for adults as well as children and computer games. They could re-edit the network series into educational and home videos. They realized the computer work could be used in a CD-I as well as on postcards, stationery and other printed materials. The list goes on. It has now become a business, which can be franchised–building on the identity which will result from publicity exposure on network television.

A Hot Title

I was recently a consultant on a feature film project. The title of the feature is absolutely captivating. It's one of those rare combinations of words that can mean lots of things to many people. The title sounds like it's talking to you. A great title like this has the ability to transcend niche markets and to reach out or cross over to many other audiences.

It was obvious, too, that the concept's creator had more in his hands than a feature. The film takes place in a Northwestern town. During location scouting, the town fathers learned about the project. They became so inspired by the film's idea and the fact it was taking place in their town, that they invested in the script development. (I believe they had a vision of a *Field of Dreams*-type phenomena occurring in their town. They wanted it to also be transformed into a tourist attraction that could draw thousands to visit.) They figured the area might sell millions of dollars in T-shirts, hotel accomodations, and food.

This was just the beginning. The title also readily lends itself to being used on beer bottles, new lines of trucks or cars, or even restaurants. The title suggested a comic strip and an illustrated book. In fact, it may be that the original idea will first be developed as a comic strip and other merchandised items and later as a feature film. By building various franchises on the value of the name, by creating national awareness through various media (be it beer, books or comics), the producer is really creating an entire business around his original concept. Whatever film they create, they are also aware that there are sequel and spin-off opportunities. If the film is not successful enough to warrant a sequel, there is still a chance for a television series. All these communication pieces work together to create a mystery, an excitement, a desire in an audience to get involved and participate through various media.

You've just read two examples of how products can be generated from an original concept. Here's how the marketing strategy too can expand to support various products. Without a way to distribute and sell your additional products, the circle from concept to market cannot be completed.

The Infomercial

This year I am producing three health-oriented infomercials. The product will be sold through long-form television advertising programs. Although I never thought I'd ever produce an infomercial (because of the negative connotations of this media form), I am finding that infomercials are an excellent marketing (and communication) device.

The program is loaded with information, and whether or not someone buys the offered product, they will walk away with something of value. (In this respect, the infomercial is only slightly different from a documentary or a how-to program. Where it is different is that it must sell product to stay on the air since that is its primary purpose.) A mystique and a desire is built up around the product that is offered for sale. If people care about their own and their family's health, they will want more information that is provided in the form of audiotapes, videos, workbooks and other printed materials.

The marketing sequence for these infomercials goes something like this. The program appears, the product is offered, and some people order. Those that do are told that they may order an additional product–for example, an audio magazine series–that is delivered at the rate of one tape per month. Since the audience for the product has been identified, there is a strong likelihood that the same people will order additional products (called an "upsell") as well. (In fact, some 20-30 percent of those who call will order the second offering.)

The product is then delivered. Once they've had a chance to use the product and realize its value, a bond is created. A few weeks later, the buyer may be sent a catalog with similar products. Again, a high percentage (up to 20 percent) of sales are made. (This far exceeds the successful one to two percent direct-mail response rate, because the mailing is a highly targeted list.) By creating an ongoing series of audiotapes (or some other form of "continuity programming"), the marketer is in touch with the consumer on a monthly basis and has the opportunity to sell other quality products. (The trust between the marketer and consumer cannot be abused.) The marketers are using infomercials as only one aspect of the marketing process, which draws out and identifies their target audience.

Recap

What you want to do is take your concept and see how many different products you can create from your core idea. The more products you can identify that have distribution channels the more revenue you will create and the greater awareness you will generate. You also want to create as many channels to your audience as you possibly can, so that you can offer multiple products. Why go to all the effort to research, produce and then sell one product when, with a well-thought out product development and marketing plan, you can expand everything you are trying to accomplish into multiple products.

Now that I've given you a free $1000 consulting session, I want something from you in return. Please use this information wisely to create products that people can really use–programs that inspire, teach and motivate. Products that benefit people's lives. If I catch you marketing something really stupid, I want the $1000 back! Now go get 'em.

SO MANY QUESTIONS, SO LITTLE TIME: PART I

Producing has two separate tracks. The "creative" track requires looking at things in new ways. The "get it done" track requires accomplishing physical steps in the right order. Asking yourself the right questions is invaluable. Use these questions. Write your own. When the questions are all answered, the project is probably done!

Were we not in so much of a hurry, there are many questions we would ask ourselves before dashing into a project. Actually, getting it done happens through asking yourself the right questions. Your own well-thought-out answers can help lay the foundation for the entire project and guide you on your way.

While writing my last book, *Film & Video Financing,* I went through chapter upon chapter of dense information on strategies about getting a production financed. What it really boils down to is finding your own palette of approaches and techniques. And these can be discovered by putting yourself through a question-driven process.

For that reason, this column and *So Many Questions: Part II* are kind of like a producer's SAT. Think about these questions, cut out this article, and paste it on your refrigerator, car dash or your new Panasonic LQ-4000 rewritable optical laserdisc recorder (Whoa! I'm starting to sound like fellow Contributing Editor Scott Billups).

The whole process of producing is finding the answers to the right questions through meeting people and asking for–and getting–support. Producing consists of a series of small steps. If you think about them beforehand, you can save a lot of time–years perhaps. That's why it's important to find out what you need by asking yourself these questions.

Before flying into action, write down answers to the questions that follow. If any remain unanswered, that means you still have preparatory work to do. Let your mind be creative in answering the questions. Write down any and all ideas. Perhaps you can use a tape recorder, then transcribe your ideas later (this prevents the act of writing from getting in the way). First time around you are in the information hunting and gathering stage, so don't be critical of the answers you get.

Go through this process more than once, and give yourself plenty of time to answer each question. By putting the questions into your subconscious, you will be working on them constantly. You may get answers at strange times, so have a scratch pad nearby to write them down. Sometimes you may not get a specific answer, but will have a subtle feeling about what to do. Pay attention, and give yourself a chance to interpret it. This can be helpful in reaching your goal. Once you've devised answers to all your questions, evaluate them.

From consulting with hundreds of producers of home videos, it is my experience that they find it difficult to be honest about the real marketplace value of their project. Producers frequently fantasize about the wealth their project will create. That's what keeps them going. However, we need to make sure that what we tell ourselves is possible. Honesty to oneself and to one's partners, investors and others is critically important.

Here are the questions. They apply mostly to home video oriented projects. But if you are working on industrials or television projects they will also be useful. Here we go.

The Project

What do I want to make?
Why do I want to make it?
What do I hope to realize in terms of financial return?
Why?
Will I be able to stick with this project for the next year? Two years? Five years?
Do I have the ability, resources and contacts to produce this project myself?

Partners

Who would be an ideal partner(s)? Why?
What kind of skills should he or she have?
What would attract him or her to this project?

Packaging and Presentation

Who are the agents that represent projects like this?
Who are the producers and others who can assist me?
Who can help me prepare a presentation? Graphics? Layout?
Who can write it?
Who can prepare financial statements and income projections?
Have I rehearsed my presentation well in front of friends before presenting it to investors?
Can I capture the interest of investors with my presentation?
What's the strongest part? The weakest? How do I know that? Is anything missing?
Do I have "letters of intent" from co-creators, writers, actors, distributors?
Do I have the following documents? Insurance policy, partnership papers, agreements with talent and creative partners.
Is my project fully packaged (script, talent, production facility, director, producer, writer, budget, schedule, commitment letters)?
What promotable elements are part of my package?

So Many Questions, So Little Time

Packaging and Presentation (Cont.)

Have I consulted with marketing and publicity experts to predetermine the hooks and promotable elements in my film or video? What are the hooks? Which hooks can be amplified? What new hooks or elements are needed?

Budgets and Rights

What will it cost?
Has my budget been professionally prepared?
Am I certain it is accurate?
Have I made assumptions about deferrals or special deals that could fall through? Did I delete them from my budget?
Have I cleared all the rights in the project (story, book, music, talent, etc.)?
Do I know the exact cost of these rights?

The Market

Is there a market for my film or video?
How do I know that?
What does my project offer that will attract a distributor?
What does my project have that will interest an audience?
What does my project have that appeals to the media and generates publicity?
Will people want to see my video more than once? Why?
What are the elements (actors, story, marketing, etc.) that will make it successful?

Income Projections

What returns can I expect?
What other videos have had similar performances?
Have I researched the market for this specific project?
Do I know the video's income potential in each market?
Do I know how revenues flow back to me from rights sales and licenses?
Do I know the deductions and fees subtracted by distributors and agents before the money reaches me?
Is there a significant upside or do expected revenues cover the budget and no more?

Development

Am I good at developing properties?

Have I the skills for developing profitable, worthwhile projects, or am I better at getting it produced once it's selected? Is there someone I can partner with who's good at development?
Do I have the time and resources to develop a property?
Should I try to raise the development money?
Do I know how risky this is?
Do I know how to structure a development deal with investors?
Am I able to incorporate promotable elements within my story or video idea? What are they?

Resources

Do I know how and where to commission key art and/or package art for my project?
What skills do I need in my support team?
Am I (or do I have) a charismatic salesperson with highly developed communication skills who can pitch the project?
Do I have a lawyer in place who can turn "letters of interest" into formal agreements?
Do I have an accountant to prepare the financial structures that are necessary?
Do I have a production company with a track record to handle the physical production of the video?
Do I have letters of intent from the principal participants that can be converted to contracts?
Do I have a financial vehicle which I can use to raise financing?
Do I have a professionally prepared budget that accurately reflects both above-the-line and below-the-line costs?
Have I examined each and every line item to find potential savings?
Have I identified the banks that finance video production?
Have I contacted the guilds and unions? Have I been able to make any special deals?
Have I found a postproduction facility that will cut a deal?
Am I willing to negotiate for everything? If not, do I have someone that is?
Have I explored deferred payments with everyone involved in the production?
Have I identified the best distributors/clients for my project?
Have I decided whether to approach them with my package, or will I wait until my video is finished? Why?
Do I know what impresses a banker? Can I make a presentation to a banker in his or her own terms and leave my normal exhilarated pitch at home?

Income Projections

Are my income projections based on similar projects? Really?
Am I able to put my desires aside and objectively assess the financial upside of my project?
Has my project been financially researched by someone experienced with each market and with how cash flows (after deductions) to the producer?

Deferrals

Who will defer some or all of his or her salary?
What are the facilities that will exchange services for equity in the project?
Where do people stand in relation to one another in the flow of revenues?
Who comes first? Who comes last? Who shares at the same level (equity partners, producers, deferrals, investors, interest, bank, loans, etc.)?

Investors

Who is willing to invest in my project?
Who–among my friends or family–will loan or invest money in it?
Who do I know that will introduce me to an investor or lender in my project?
Can my lawyer, family, co-producer or others refer me to potential investors?
Who has supported my work in the past?
What former employers will help in my financing search?
Do I know a banker that will loan money?
Can I borrow against my equity in a house or property?
Are there companies within or without the video business interested in participating in some manner in this project?
Are there corporate sponsors I can approach?
Are there manufacturers, airlines or service companies that may donate or invest by providing the production with equipment, airline tickets, hotels, food, clothes, cars, etc.?
Do I know a lawyer who will work for equity in the project?
Are there any blocks between me and the money I need to raise? What are they? What do I need to do to make those blocks go away? Am I willing to do it?

International Pre-Sale Agents

Which distributors have handled similar videos?
Who are they? In the U.S., Europe, Asia?
Will they pre-buy rights?
Historically, what income have they generated, what advances or pre-buy payments and deals have they made?
What producers were involved in these deals? (Have I found and talked with them? What was their advice?)
Is my attorney watching over the project and all negotiations?
Do I need to make pre-sales in order to fully or partially finance my project?
Have I found a reputable foreign sales agent?
Is he or she someone I feel good about working with on my project?
Does he or she attend all the major video markets?
What kind of sales record has the agent generated for his other producers?
Am I confident my sales agent knows the major foreign buyers, and isn't simply sub-licensing through other agents?
Do I have a trailer, key art or other materials my sales agent can use?
Have I explored domestic pay television, satellite companies, and pay-per-view for financing?
Does my project really have value in the foreign markets? Why?

Obviously, some of these questions will not apply to your specific projects, but I'll bet they made you think more deeply about your projects than usual. Most of us wait until the last minute to think about things that actually require some serious thought long before we charge into production. I hope these questions sparked your thinking.

Next month, we'll continue the adventure. Until then, go get 'em.

SO MANY QUESTIONS, SO LITTLE TIME: PART II

Here are some of the questions we should ask ourselves before dashing into a new project. In fact, I've learned that getting a production done is really the result of asking yourself the right questions. The path from program development through production and marketing is basically a series of small steps, each of which needs care and attention.

These questions can help you with the answers and resources you will need for your project. If you think about them now, and answer them thoughtfully, you'll be in much better shape as you move forward. Give it a try.

Risk Capital

Am I offering a fair deal to my investors?
Is it competitive with other investments they could make?
Am I aware of how important my own integrity, enthusiasm, and ability to create a vision are in obtaining investments?
Are my investors also in the video business and can they help get distribution?
Do I know what my investors really want?
Do I have more investors lined up than I really need? If not, then why?
Can I get the names of potential investors for every "no" I receive?
Has my lawyer explained state laws and SEC regulations about raising money to me?
Do I understand how limited partnerships work?
Have I structured my deal in a competitive and equitable fashion?
Do I understand how letters of credit work?
Is it desirable to have someone else raise money for me? Why? Why not?
Have I prepared a "hit list" of potential investors?
Am I willing to network with virtually everyone I come into contact with in my life?
What am I doing to get visibility for my project?
Are there television, home video, corporations, or other buyers that might want an equity position in my project?
Have I found a foreign sales agent?
How many markets do I wish to pre-sell to finance my production?
What markets will give me an upside?
Have I identified co-production partners?

Pre-Sales

What is my pre-sale strategy?
Is there really an opportunity for pre-selling rights in my video? Why?
What percent of my budget can I really expect to raise?
Have I found a reputable pre-sale agent?

Pre-Sales (Cont.)

How long has he or she been in business?
Have I pre-sold domestic pay television?
Do I have a U.S. distributor in place?
Do I understand how cash flows back to me from the sales agent?
Do I understand how revenues from distribution come back to me?
Deductions?

Distribution

Is it my best strategy to engage the financing and support of a distributor
before production or when the video is finished? Why?
Is it realistic to think a video distributor will "pick up" my video once it's
finished?
Who might? Why?
What is the greatest advance I can expect to get from the distributor?
Why do I think that?
What have these companies recently paid for other similar videos?
Who will negotiate my deal with a distributor, financiers, and/or
investors–a lawyer, a producer's rep, or me?
Are they experienced?
Who will negotiate special deals like sponsorship, facilities deals,
deferments?
Are they experienced?
Are my negotiation skills strong enough?
Am I, or is someone else, able to conceive all the financial elements
necessary to put my project together?
Can all the pieces be tailored to fit financially and legally, and can I still
offer my investors (if any) an attractive return? (Am I able to clearly map
out this strategy?)
Have I found investors, actors, facilities, distributors, and others–all of
whom have a real stake in my project–who can continue to promote the
video to ensure profits once the video is completed?
Are my deals with my distributors equitable?
Is everyone appropriately awarded for the risks they have taken or will take?

Financing

Have I taken the time to design a strategy, game plan, and "hit list" for my
financing efforts?
What do I think the best route or combination of routes is? Why?
Are my partners strong, and do they really bring something to the party?
Are my attorney and accountants experienced in the video business?
Is my investor deal appealing?
Does it communicate that I'm looking out for my investor's interest?

Resources

Do I get good feelings from the people involved in this project?
Do I expect that we will work well together?
Do they have something special to contribute?
Are our skills complementary or supplementary?
Can other people I've met better handle these jobs?
If I know someone isn't "right" for a project, am I willing to move him or her off of it?
Do I have an agent that can help me secure actors?

Home Video

Who are the best distributors for my video? Why?
What elements in my video are particularly attractive to distributors? Why? Is my budget appropriate to the genre and the expected revenue potential of my video? Why?
Does my video meet the expectations of its audience?
Is there a strong script?
On what schedule is the production budget paid out?
What are the basic contract terms in a home video contract?
What am I looking for?
What kind of deal do I want?
What rights am I specifically not granting to a particular distributor? Why? What are realistic home video revenues?
How do I calculate them?
Over what period of time will I receive them?
What is the retail price?
How does retail price affect royalties?
Is there a best time to release my video?
In what territories world-wide does my video have the most potential? Why?
Do I know exactly what delivery materials I must submit to the distributor before I get paid?
Are there any conflicting holdbacks that will keep me from releasing my video for a period of time?
Do I have the rights to all the rights required by my video?
When do I expect royalty reports and royalty checks?

Video Sponsorship

What's more important to me: getting production funds or a marketing commitment? Why?
What are sponsors looking for?
What are the benefits my project can offer a sponsor?
What can I give to a sponsor?

31

Video Sponsorship (Cont.)

What are all the things I might want from a sponsor?
How could a sponsor use my video?
Can I justify and calculate the number of consumer impressions my video will deliver? How?
What companies could use my video as a premium? How?
Do I have contacts with an advertising or product placement agency?
Why does the value of my project increase to a distributor when I have a sponsor attached?
What makes my video sponsorable?
Can I create a different version of my video for a sponsor?
How can I do this?
How can I create a second distribution window after a premium deal window expires?
Do I have the time to find and conclude a sponsor deal?
What are some marketing ideas for my video?
Who are the target audiences? How does the video serve them?
Are there manufacturers whose products can be included in my video?
How can they use my video in their promotions or sales presentations?
What is its value to them?
What would they be willing to pay or provide?

Summary

Do I have the energy necessary to make this video? Am I able to deal with rejection? Is my intent strong enough to go through everything it will take to make this video? What will sustain me as I find the answers and carry out the actions associated with these questions? Why do I want to make this video? (Spend at least an hour answering this question. You may be surprised by the answers you find.) Write down or record the answers no matter how silly or profound they may be at the time. Go back to your list of answers one week later and see if you can find the real answer in your list–one that you can look to in the months to come for strength and inspiration.

Good luck and much success in your search for financing. Now go get 'em!

PRODUCTION

THE BALI SHOOT

I have long had the dream of being able to record my experiences without any gear whatsoever. This article is about taking the smallest high-quality camera I could find (at the time) to a faraway magical location. Was it possible with minimal effort to record my experiences? You bet!

Are there advantages in using low cost, high-end consumer Video 8 cameras for documentary production? That's what I was trying to find out late last year, when I borrowed a CCD-9 camera from Sony and two wireless microphones (one professional, one consumer) from Nady Systems to take on location to Bali, Indonesia. I planned to shoot a travel series pilot there.

I've produced many video and film documentaries. Like other producers, I've learned that whenever you bring lots of gear into a shoot the logistics can suddenly become more important than the subject matter. The things you want to shoot have to wait until you are set up for them. But with Video 8, I didn't have to worry about such things as white balance before shooting. Not having to give the camera much attention meant no one else did either, making it inconspicuous.

I Passed For a Tourist

I've made many trips to Bali during the last 20 years, so I knew to a great extent who and what I wanted to tape, and, to some degree, the conditions I would encounter. I had taken 16mm cameras into that country a decade ago, which caused quite a stir. Normally you need a press pass, and then are assigned a government liaison to make sure you don't film any bare breasts. This time I wanted to enter like a tourist, even though I had 40 rolls of Video 8 cassettes on me. Fortunately that tape is small, and I was able to spread it through my luggage, put it in my pockets, and pretty much hide all 40 hours of raw stock. Imagine trying to do that with 16mm film!

Rather than hide the camera during the customs process, I shot as we went through it. I taped the guards, the immigration officials, and, when our luggage came off the plane, the customs inspector. He was so self-conscious about being videotaped that he concentrated on making sure he looked official. He gave everything a cursory look, but didn't think to question my camera. Later, I saw many tourists with video cameras, and realized why he thought nothing of mine. (Perhaps my anxiety comes from working in New York and Los Angeles, where you need a permit to shoot professionally in your own home!)

Accompanying me was Geraldine Overton, a CBS staff photographer (now also my wife), who specializes in portraiture of television stars. Besides occasionally shooting Video 8 herself, she took stills that I planned to incorporate into the video program.

Sometimes we took a tripod; I later wished we had used it more often. It is extremely difficult to hold the Video 8 camera steady. It's so lightweight, only 3 or 4 lbs. with batteries. Unlike VHS cameras, it doesn't balance on your shoulder. A tripod is needed especially for panning. An amateur Steadicam JR for such cameras was introduced after my trip; I wish I'd had one with me.

I developed a hand-held technique for interviews when I didn't have a tripod. I started by composing a slightly wide head shot of my subject, and then while still shooting moved the camera away from me so that I could maintain eye contact with that person, keeping them relaxed. Occasionally I would look back into the camera to make sure it was level, making adjustments if necessary.

We also took a reflector, which twisted down into a large pizza-size carrying case. The villages in Bali are surrounded by high trees and dense foliage, and the midday equatorial light is dreadful. The reflector gave us a fill light when the sun was high.

Do's and Don'ts

I learned many things about shooting Video 8 through my experimentation. Turn off the automatic focus function. If there is something in the foreground and you are panning foliage, the automatic focus will go crazy–shifting back and forth with every move. The only time I used the automatic focus was in low-light situations where it was impossible to focus, and when I knew that there would be no other objects that would throw off the focusing function.

In many instances, I left the automatic iris on. If the subject was backlit, I switched to manual to expose the subject and not the background. This is very hard to do correctly, especially if you are trying to match scenes within a sequence. The adjustments looked good through the viewfinder. However when I returned to Los Angeles and replayed some of the scenes, I learned that some were either under-exposed or overexposed. Perhaps a larger portable color monitor on location would have afforded me greater accuracy.

Here are some additional do's and don'ts:

- Although the camera is superb at shooting in low light, it will look decent only on the original tape. If you try to transfer or dub it down during editing, it will loose all color and appear very grainy. Nevertheless, the low-light ability of the camera can be a bit seductive. I shot classic Balinese nighttime shadow puppet performances, sitting directly beside the puppeteer as he worked his "actors" against a shadow screen. The sole illumination was from an oil lamp a foot or so above his head. This dim light, however, was sufficient to capture the audience, performing puppets, puppeteers and musicians in silhouette as I alternately shot from in front of and behind the screen.

- Shoot primarily close-ups and medium shots. Long shots won't hold detail unless they have strong graphic elements.

- Compose scenes with bright primary colors. This will focus the viewer's attention. Beef up your shot through strong colors and contrast.

- Again, beware backlit situations. The camera will read the background, so use the manual iris to correctly expose your subject's face.

- Keep your subject close to the camera when shooting dialogue scenes for maximum sound quality. I had some problems with the wireless microphones, so I really didn't get the chance to see what they could do.

- Carry the camera so that it can be pulled out and turned on quickly. I used a woven basket backpack. In five seconds, I could be rolling. Sometimes I just carried the camera by its superbly designed hand strap. One day we climbed Mt. Batur, a volcano. We started in the dark at 4 a.m. with the camera recording only the sound of our huffs and puffs. It was hard enough to get ourselves up the side of the volcano, and that's when I appreciated how lightweight the camera is. My Video 8 tapes were one hour long. Each day, the camera, a few batteries, and two extra tapes were all I needed. In only a few instances, where I shot performances or rituals that were hours long, did I need more than one tape per day.

- The camera's automatic functions, low weight, and ease of operation enable anyone to be your "second unit." I let local folks do some shooting so I could include myself in certain scenes. In typical *60 Minutes* style, locals shot profiles or over-the-shoulder shots which I could eventually use as cutaways.

Can I Charge It?

Batteries were a major problem and a source of frustration. The international battery charger I brought took all night to charge a 30-minute battery and died after a few days. Our major concern was always whether we'd have enough power. I met a Frenchman who also had a Sony Video 8 camera, and he graciously took my 45-minute battery which is twice as heavy as a 30-minute version and charged it overnight. I tried to buy his charger but to no avail.

I finally found a 20 lb. device that converted Indonesian power to the U.S. standard, which was too big to carry with us. I used the device with my U.S. battery charger, and we would leave it in a bamboo house with electricity. This allowed me to charge a battery or two a day. Since I took four or five batteries with me, I would make sure they were all charged before heading out for extended trips. Batteries gave about two to three hours' worth of power, and they never lasted as long as the manufacturers claimed. Not using the automatic zoom or focus, by the way, saves power.

The camera, meanwhile, held up very well. I was sorry I couldn't get the wireless microphones to work. I don't know whether this was a function of the particular equipment I had, or if I just didn't test them well enough. There were situations where I really needed them. For example, recording dialogue in long shot showing two people in a crowded, noisy market was impossible. You had to be on top of the camera to be heard.

Upon returning to the States, I used a Video 8 VTR to transfer to Betacam selected scenes from 12 hours of tape. The resulting five hours of time-coded Betacam became my masters. I transferred this to 3/4" with time-code on window dubs, and edited it. The audio held up remarkably well. The video usually did too, unless it was poorly exposed, shaky, or shot with low-light.

Technically speaking, the most successful sequence was of women harvesting rice. Our presence made little difference to them. I was able to cover their work from every angle, including holding the camera high above their heads as they separated the rice from the chaff by beating it against boards. At 7 a.m., the light was excellent. The women wore bright colors, and the sound was great. All conditions were optimal.

In contrast, one of the most memorable moments in Bali made for unsuccessful images. We were at a special religious ceremony where village priests performed rites by which ancestral spirits blessed newborns. Incense smoke spiraled up toward a full moon. Women chanted and a gamelan orchestra (whose music I describe below) played gently in the background. Villagers sat beneath huge altars adorned with offerings and prayed while priests sprinkled water on them.

The only light sources were a single incandescent tube located high in one of the altars, flaming incense, and the full moon. Although I could capture all the images, there wasn't enough light to make it through the transfer process. The addition of a small camera light would have helped, but would have been inappropriate. The secret of such shoots is striking a balance between ideal technical conditions and being invisible and unobtrusive.

By the way, gamelan music indigenous to Indonesia includes the deep low tones of gongs and the high-pitched sound of flutes. Its dynamic range can be difficult to record without distortion, but it came out remarkably well on Video 8's audio track.

The Future

About half of what I shot under the best of conditions was acceptable quality for broadcast. My next trip to exotic lands will include some lights, a portable generator for charging batteries, the Steadicam JR and I hope a Hi8 camera. More gear will probably mean adding another person to the crew, which will impact on what is being documented. Nevertheless, these added elements are important to get professional quality.

Another key ingredient to this kind of production is low-cost, high quality graphics and effects. In terms of basic shooting, however, my Bali experiment proved to me that the Video 8 format, properly used under ideal conditions, offers major advantages for documentary production. It's an essential piece of the desktop video puzzle.

ZEN & THE ART OF STEADICAM JR

I returned to Bali and Java with a remarkable piece of gear (we videographers do love gear) which I hoped would bring a transcendental quality to my subject matter and allow me to spend less time shooting and more time just "be-ing." It worked.

It was a whole new kind of visual language. I had a sense of freedom, unrestrained movement, and a spirit-like point of view, and I knew that the tape I was shooting would convey it all. Moving with a Canon Hi8 A-1 Mark II mounted on a Steadicam JR, I walked around the world's largest Ninth Century Buddhist monument, and shot its 400 life-size Buddhas and nearly two miles of bas-reliefs depicting the life of the Enlightened One.

I was on a trip to Java and Bali. Although I'd been to Bali frequently since 1970, this time had special significance. Not only was I there to try out the Steadicam JR, but also to find adventure and capture some compelling video. Geraldine, my wife, is a photographer. Each day we would plan what we hoped to shoot, but often we wound up simply going on impromptu adventures with friends–Indonesian painters, shadow puppeteers, or shaman.

Steadicam JR is a wonderfully designed gadget, specially created for lightweight camcorders. It took some time to initially rig the camera to the Steadicam platform, even though the instructions are very thorough. Maybe it's because the camera and rig just feel so darn strange at first–even when they're balanced correctly.

Los Angeles-based Cinema Products Corporation manufactures and sells Steadicam JR. They also supply a terrific padded case for it that will also fit the camera you choose to mount on it. Although I thought it would take some time getting the rig unfolded, plugged in, and turned on, it really wasn't bad–15 seconds and I was rolling. I incorrectly assumed that once you get the camera balanced you're set. Instead I found that you do have to tweak the rig occasionally, which is painless. One hand holds the camera and the other gently turns or tilts a small ring under the base of the platform that floats the camera in the intended direction. The human body and arms do the rest. It is a great adventure to be able to keep both eyes open and see everything around you while also viewing and composing your shots on the rig's liquid crystal display (LCD), rather than squinting one-eyed through a viewfinder as you try not to stumble.

The Tai Chi movements I learned years ago suddenly came in handy. "Ward off with right hand," "stork spreads wings," and "carry tiger to the mountain" far better describe the kinds of Steadicam moves you can make than "pan left and tilt" ever could. I never did, however, get very comfortable with the toggle switch in front of the handgrip that turns the camera on and off. I frequently bounced the shot trying to stop tape. At four pounds, the Canon A-1 Mark II is about the heaviest camcorder that will go on a Steadicam JR–allowing only a small battery. I thought this might be a severe handicap but it turned out not to be. Initially, as with every new mount, there is the tendency to try to move too fast, which I did. (Look ma, no hands!)

The nice thing about the Steadicam JR is that it gives you the ability to get more involved with the activity you are shooting. For one thing, people can see your face and you don't have to look at the screen all the time. Documentary purists believe that success is measured by how little your camera influences what you are shooting. They know that the act of observing affects the observed. Others, however, have no qualms about "directing" and manipulating documentaries. I draw from both schools, but feel I've discovered the seedlings of yet another approach. I'm not quite sure I'd recommend it for producing "traditional" documentaries or industrials, but I do feel this approach can reveal profound personal insights.

Steadicam JR lets you participate. Video has the same effect that Polaroids had in primitive cultures–instant feedback. Often a small group gathered behind me to watch the images on the magical LCD. Once all my subjects ended up behind the camera, resulting in an empty scene!

Even though Steadicam lets you participate, you still must make a choice about what and what not to tape. And since you are experiencing and recording simultaneously, you don't always know if what you are shooting has any long-term value. Part of you must think so, however, or you wouldn't be pushing the button. Consider: What we chose to shoot we automatically imbue with meaning. Further meaning comes in post, selecting, editing and juxtaposing our recordings of reality. This is the part where we try to make sense of it all.

One technique I experimented with to capture impressions of Bali and Java was writing down daily incidents and moments as if they were a dream. The important thing was to take this attitude when recording these experiences. Often we may not understand their meaning and value until we've turned these gems over in our minds and let every facet reflect.

"Something here invites the unconscious to come out with great intensity," I wrote. "I feel it every time I'm here. There is a thin membrane between dream and reality. Sometimes you are not quite sure what side you are on. Reality is our own selection of images projected on our own internal screen. Our unconscious feeds our inner projector with images that instruct and call attention to what we need to learn. Sometimes we are not always paying attention, so we'll have to sit through the same experience again to get it."

In using Steadicam JR, I gave up the sense of distance I get when looking through a camera. I entered reality with both eyes wide open. The establishing shot is an objective shot, a kind of "witness," which tells us where we are going. If you think–"oh, I've been too tight, I better make an establishing shot," you've just lost it. You are no longer in the experience.

In a foreign country, the senses can often be overwhelmed. Everything is alive and seems relevant. With newness, there is no desire to filter out what you are seeing. Nothing is taken for granted, it's all important, and it all comes rushing in. The mind tries to process and record it all. You are awake like never before–eyes burning, ears ringing, skin tingling, nose aroused, and heart pumping. Everything is happening right now.

When I was a young filmmaker, I had hoped to make my living by recording and sharing my experiences. Using Steadicam JR returned me to that feeling. It goes where you go. Sometimes you follow it, but it's very difficult to synthesize and organize what you are shooting as you go. This is especially true when you are a stranger in a strange land, and you don't know what's happening next. If you are shooting a "how-to-change-a-tire video," you could easily edit it in the camera. That's because you already know how to organize the material. Life's not like that, it doesn't unfold in neat three-act plays.

What if we let the Steadicam JR float into the experience guided by the unconscious, and we just followed? Don't think, don't pre-edit, just be. A Zen approach to Steadicam taping. To shoot successfully you have to "be." You have to let go into the experience. When you do, remarkable things happen. My ideas in this area were encouraged recently while screening the first episode of a PBS series for Spring '92, titled *Millennium.*

I loved the show, specifically because the narrator struggled to make sense of his own journey amid alien cultures, and to discover indigenous tribes and their wisdom. It appeared as if much of what "just happened" was taped and later edited to make sense, but there really wasn't much of a "story." He was thrown off-balance, and so was the viewer. I felt this was a very honest approach. You come away from this program with disturbing questions that haunt you the next day.

That off-center feeling is what it was like to be in Java and Bali. Not everything I wrote down was covered by Steadicam footage, but combining those images with narration will reveal many things. The piece still needs to be edited. I am like a tightrope walker, shooting with a Steadicam JR, trying to refine the process. Now it's your turn. Shoot and let me know what you find out. Until then, go get 'em.

WHAT DO EXECUTIVE PRODUCERS DO, ANYWAY? PART I

I started my career in the trenches (writing, shooting and editing). In this article, I am probably trying to figure out what I've been doing during many of the last few years.

<u>Do they get the money? Do they put in their own money? Just what do executive producers do, anyway?</u> Nobody really seems to know the answer to this question (except perhaps executive producers and they aren't talking). The executive producer credit is usually prominently displayed first (or last) in a video production; no doubt they're important folks.

We know what the producer and director do, they produce and direct. But the whole art of executive producing is rather mysterious, so let's shed some light on it.

Meta-Management

Executive producing is the art of "meta-management." I use <u>meta</u> in the sense of its dictionary definition of "standing above or behind," the way an executive producer stands behind the producer and director.

Besides obtaining the money (however that happens!), there are other aspects to the executive producer's job. The most important of these is people. And whenever there are people, there are relationships. The management of these relationships falls into the executive producer's domain. This is also true of directors and producers, but for executive producers it's on another level–the level of meta-management.

The executive producer is responsible for all the key relationships. On one side, you have the business relationships between financiers, facilities, distributors, marketers and broadcasters. On the other side, you have creative relationships. The executive producer may hire the producer, director and writer. The concept for the program may be something that the executive producer found or developed. The executive producer is often the first person to get the project financed, fully packaged and made. (In some instances, producers bring their packages to executive producers to get them made.)

In my most recent work, I developed concepts with a broadcaster. Some originated with the broadcaster; others I found. Some we selected, developed and then "green-lighted" for production together.

Money, Money, Money

People in our business can't seem to say the <u>M</u> word enough. When we say that the executive producer "handles the money," what does that mean? It means that he or she <u>is responsible</u> for the money. It doesn't necessarily mean that the executive producer puts up the money. Rather, the executive producer is responsible for the project's financial status and for delivering the program on time and within budget. For this, of course, he or she looks to and depends on other people.

Since you depend on other people, as a producer I've learned that it's very important to make sure that all the agreements are in place. This is also the executive producer's job, but again at a meta-level. Without agreements people get crazy. I know you know what I mean. We've all been in situations where agreements weren't clear. We know how terrible that feels. All the energy goes into thinking about who's getting what.

The first thing I do is create clear, written agreements with my creative partners in projects. These agreements are usually a short letter or deal memo (which may later be expanded into a long-form agreement) stipulating what the project is, each partner's responsibilities, fees, payment terms (usually triggered by performance), credits and profit participation (if any). When people start to work on a project and things aren't spelled out for them, they may feel they are on very thin ice. This makes for very insecure and inauspicious beginnings. The first thing an executive producer does is clarify the relationship in basic terms: money, money, money. Once done, there's a sigh of relief, and the creative work begins wholeheartedly.

I don't often get into the fine points (in legal jargon the <u>boilerplate</u>) of an employment or rights acquisition contract. That's for the lawyers to do. And they may go back and forth for days, weeks, or months. That's their job, and I want no part of it. I want my relationship with the director, actor, or producer to be "creative." And so do they. You can't be negotiating with someone out of one side of your mouth, while trying to instill inspiration, confidence and security out of the other.

Nevertheless, the executive producer is called in for things that others deem as unpleasant—such as negotiating, or renegotiating, or simply saying what needs to be said. I've been held up (as in "this is a hold up") by disgruntled facilities and freelance directors. Misunderstandings about money are common in our business. Here are some variations on a theme that executive producers frequently encounter. And it's always about money, money, money.

A shoot or postproduction schedule runs longer than anticipated. Even though the original employment deal was a "buyout" (a flat fee for the entire project), the director (non-union) wants more money. The director took more time than expected, then held up the video masters as leverage (until he was advised by his lawyer otherwise). An out-of-town production facility and staff producer didn't get along. The producer refused to pay for poor quality work. The facility was not going to send the camera originals until they got a check significantly larger than what was agreed upon.

The producer in both cases left the job incomplete. <u>Call in the executive producer</u>! I refused to be held up for ransom. But I did agree to be fair and that we'd work out an agreement we could both live with. And I'd do it fast. But only after the masters were returned. How do you do this?

You have to get into the head of the party that feels wronged. I've been there, so I know what they are feeling. They are scared they are going to get burned. The first order of business is to assure them through your own personal integrity that they will not. I say something like this:

"Look, the first thing I want you to do is return our tapes by Federal Express. When you've done that, call me back and I'll be here to renegotiate your fee. I'll probably pay you most of your overages (over budget items), but you'll have to justify the expenses to me. You'll probably get less than what you're asking for, however, but I'll end up paying more than what was agreed at the outset. We'll both give up something. The hassle we're having now will go away, and we'll both feel good about the outcome."

It works when you set up a context for both people to agree. Both parties <u>do</u> agree, and disputes are settled. From this foundation of trust, it's not uncommon for people to work together again.

I am unwilling for messes to persist for very long; I don't like the feeling. I was willing to go to the effort, however uncomfortable, so that the party that was feeling wronged (for whatever reason) wouldn't be hurt financially and we'd get closure right away. Even though things had gone askew and there was some misunderstanding, we'd both come out of it with a good feeling. To have a successful career in video, you want to create good will and long-term relationships.

To accomplish that I had to not only know my needs, but the other person's as well. This comes from knowing what you want. You can't get it if you don't know what it is. Then, somehow (naturally), the getting comes rather easily. You may have to guide, teach, cajole or demand. But you know what you want and need and can communicate that to others, you'll get it.

Don't Cross This Line

There is a line, however, which is not to be crossed that I am learning about and have experienced recently. That line has to do with where the executive producer's job starts and stops before it enters someone else's sphere of responsibility. If you hire a producer, then the producer's job is to produce. If an executive producer has to step into producing (or directing or writing or whatever), then this is an acknowledgment that they've hired incorrectly. The first job of the executive producer is to hire correctly. If you don't do it correctly, it's time to get another day job.

When you've hired someone, you've already agreed on what they will do. Their domain has been established. You have to live with that decision unless things really go off track. Otherwise, you have to back off. Your job is now to be as supportive as possible, and to bring your talents, abilities and insights into play only when they are required or requested. But, most of the time, you don't want them to be required.

That was a hard one for me to understand. "What do you mean you don't want to hear from me?" screamed my wounded ego. "Because, you dummy, you've already hired the best people to deliver the goods. It's not your job," I replied.

I frequently want to do something, just to make sure I still can. But that's not doing the job I have now. Now I realize, "If you want to direct, then direct!" Executive producing is not the place to be confused about what hat to wear.

To be continued. . .

Meanwhile, raise some money and executive-produce. Now go get 'em!

WHAT DO EXECUTIVE PRODUCERS DO, ANYWAY? PART II

In the last article, we discussed the mysterious art of executive producing and the responsibilities of managing people, money and relationships, of creating agreements, and of production intervention. Now there's more!

Setting Limits

The executive producer has the final word. He or she is responsible for every aspect of the production and is held accountable to his or her employers, be they broadcasters, home video companies or corporate entities. Every project has restrictions, which may relate to budgets, schedules, formats or content. The executive producer (and everyone who works with him or her) must also conform to these limitations. The limits must be clearly defined for everyone. If you or your employees ignore these limitations, you won't work again. They'll take away your "executive producer card," since you are the one your employer hired to keep everything on track.

Giving Rope

Concurrent with the role the executive producer is asked to play in "limiting" the perimeters is another role that requires that the producer get the greatest contribution possible out of the cast and crew.

I try to give the people who work with me a lot of room, lots of rope. This has been difficult to do sometimes because I also want to feel in control of my projects. Yet I also want to see how much responsibility someone can handle.

I've been given jobs where I had lots of responsibility. I've had jobs where I wasn't given any. In the former, my bosses got ten times what they paid me. In the latter case, they got no more than what they required. Most people who work in our business do so because they like work that allows them to express their creativity as fully as possible.

If you let people do more, they will, and if managed the project's quality will exceed its budgetary price tag. Ours is not factory work. In fact, it may be one of the last businesses in the country where there is still a work ethic. People in our business care about the quality of their work and will deliver quality because their own integrity calls for it (regardless of what they're paid). Producers, directors, writers, crews and actors want to excel. They want to create a "break" for themselves, and want the chance to really perform. When I've got funding for a project, I'm delighted to offer an opportunity. I know that if I give creative people their shot, nine times out of ten their work will go beyond my expectations. If you allow people more responsibility than they've had, you have the chance to really see them do something terrific. If you confine them, the results will be restricted. Your employer doesn't care about how you get the job done or what philosophy you use. They want results. As an executive producer, you have to deliver, on time and on budget.

This means you have to trust your people and to communicate clearly what the limitations are. And at the same time, you must trust them to do more, to give more, and to produce the greatest results they can. An executive producer has to be prepared, from time to time, to pull everyone back, to remind them of the limitations. It's not a free-for-all. (Sometimes you have to yell "Stop!" If you don't, you'll still be working on it on the due date.)

Interventions

On one occasion, I had to intervene against a director's wishes after three days of shooting. We were out of tape and drop-dead tired. The crew had long gone home, and it was time to return the gear to the rental house. The director was holding onto my pant leg begging for "one more shot," as I dragged him out of the studio in the harsh reality of dawn. It broke my heart, but I had to say, "I'm sorry, but we're finished now."

Another time I required a producer to cancel several days of new shooting because I felt we had more than enough already in the can to finish a terrific show. I suggested we edit what we had and then see if we needed more. We didn't.

The Creative Process

The most important thing to realize about other people is that we all see things very, very differently. I mean that in the extreme. We take it for granted that just because we speak English we understand what everyone means. This is not so. This assumption can lead to enormous problems and frustration. If you start with the premise that humans perceive things very differently, then you can at least try to understand how other people think and work.

Creative Differences

Prior to most voice-recording sessions, you prepare a script. Then you go into the studio, and you follow the script. On one occasion when the talent also had final creative control of the project, the talent refused to use the script even though that person had a hand in writing it. The talent said, "I can't work this way. I have to see how I feel, and then just do it." No amount of cajoling was going to move that mountain. The path of least resistance was to go along with it. I could see that this was the way the talent worked, and that this was the way it was going to be. As executive producer, I had to relax and support the talent in being creative in the studio regardless of my own feelings that most people do not work this way and that it is very expensive. My role was to create a supportive environment so that we could get the best material from the session as possible.

Another example: The director is also the interviewer on a documentary. The show has already been rough-cut prior to the host shoot. We are to shoot a few lines of interstitial material with the host, which will connect the various segments. The cameras start rolling. Instead of going through the script, starting with the first paragraph and moving forward, the director begins interviewing the host. We are not getting any material that's been written! Twenty minutes later, I find a moment to interrupt. I ask the director to join me out of the room, away from the host and crew. I ask the director why no script material is being recorded and to please get to the script. I don't want improvisation. The director is enormously upset and defensive. The director said my interruption sabotaged a strategy the director was using to relax the host, and build up that person's confidence. She said we were getting what we needed anyway, even though it wasn't written. I disagreed. I said that not only was the host (an amateur) as relaxed as she was going to get, but that none of the material was usable as it did not fit into our approach to the documentary. The director didn't seem to hear me. I figured I'd really blown it. Not only were we not getting what we needed, but I had sent the director into an angry rage. Within minutes of returning to the cameras, the director started working on the script. We got what was written.

I'm still second-guessing myself on this one. Rarely do I interrupt shoots. Here I felt compelled to do so. Did I overstep my bounds? The director became enormously upset and felt betrayed. Yet I didn't believe we were going to get what we needed, so I intervened. That's the executive producer's prerogative. Sometimes you use it. Sometimes it's unpleasant.

Yet another example of how differently people work and think. I came to a documentary shoot to see how things were going. The director knew exactly what he wanted–in fact to such a degree that it was staggering. Not only had he previsualized every scene, but he knew exactly how much footage to shoot at the head of a scene for a voiceover. And he knew what he wanted the voiceover to say and how long it would run. He knew how he would cut it, he knew exactly what to shoot, and that's what he was doing. He was not overshooting coverage "just in case." I'm rarely that clear on how everything will go together, so I shoot somewhat more coverage. What he was doing was going so well there was nothing for me to do–so I left.

The executive producer is not the director, nor the producer. So the executive producer is not to direct or produce, but rather manage the work of the producer and director in the most supportive role as possible.

Here are some goals for executive producers to hold in mind:

- Cast the right people for the right jobs and as part of a team.

- Make sure abilities are complementary and not supplementary.

- Get as much creative work out of people as possible.

- Keep the team spirit alive.

- Give people "creative rope" when it will enhance the project.

- Make people feel good about what they are doing.

- Smooth the path for everyone. Play a supportive role.

- Be a leader and the final arbitrator. Provide the last word.

- Be the liaison between the financial, marketing and production groups.

- Anticipate problems and solutions.

- Hold the vision of the entire project from start to finish.

- Make sure the program is consistent with marketing and promotion goals.

- Learn how much or how little to be around.

Until next time, go get 'em.

PRODUCING TO MAKE A DIFFERENCE

In the beginning of my career, I felt the power of film and wanted to use it responsibly. Over 25 years later, I am still struggling to do meaningful, contributory work with the skills I've acquired. The greater my commitment to do quality work, the more possible it is.

Younger videographers take note: Stick with your original dream. It is possible! You may not get there in the first year, or the second year, or even the second decade of your career, but you will get there. Therefore it's important to choose subjects worthy of your time and effort.

This month I am deviating from my usual focus on marketing, distribution and financing. With this column, I thought it might be appropriate for us to reflect on what we hope to achieve with our experience, technical skills and financial resources.

When I started making films (you remember them) at art school in the mid-Sixties, I saw film's potential to take us into altered states of consciousness, and to make social and political change. I told myself that I'd never make a TV commercial. And for more than ten years that was so.

In 1978, I made *Dolphin*, an hour-long documentary on interspecies communication between humans and dolphins that made a plea to end dolphin slaughters. Although it was shown on 33 networks throughout the world and at an International Whaling Commission meeting, it was only in recent years that Starkist and Bumble Bee promised not to buy tuna that was caught in a manner that killed dolphins. I felt a great sense of victory, and although there's certainly more work to be done about gill nets, I wrote my investors about the triumph and thanked them for their support.

But then my work took an unexpected turn in the Eighties. I got tired of the up and down (mostly down) emotional and financial curve of independent life. I was lucky to produce one independent short or feature documentary each year, and my learning curve was directly tied to these few projects. I wasn't learning unless I was producing and trying out new things. To top it off, someone sent me their resume listing hundreds of commercials and films they'd worked on. "Incredible," I thought. "Is this possible? Think of the learning!"

So I got some real jobs and went down paths I had no idea I'd ever pursue. I produced dozens of superficial segments for variety television. I produced nearly 100 political campaign spots for senatorial and gubernatorial races. I filled Showtime/The Movie Channel's pay-TV air with over 1200 promotional segments. At Vestron Video, I acquired, produced and/or developed more than 200 home video programs. That's a lot of product! I ended up replicating the resume I was so impressed by as an independent. But other than that, what did I have to put on my reel? Not much that made me feel really proud.

On the other hand, the learning was fantastic. I spent tens of millions of dollars of other people's money learning. But the end result was simply a lot of entertaining stuff, a lot of persuasive and promotional programming.

When I think back, however, I am still most fond of *Dolphin*. Why? Because the result had some impact in saving dolphin lives. I feel this way although *Dolphin* still hasn't repaid all its investors after ten years, and Vestron Video programs have grossed over $60 million. My Vestron programs were basically diversionary entertainment. Other than the *National Geographic* programs, most don't seem to make a difference.

Since Vestron and Showtime weren't arenas where I could "produce to make a difference," I had to find other outlets for that side of myself. I did that through writing, lecturing and participating in organizations outside work. But I was divided and living two lives. My desire to contribute and my desire to earn a living were not integrated. (I knew visionary engineer Buckminster Fuller quite well before he died. I once asked him how to integrate one's ideals and work. I saw the enormous contributions he'd made, and he seemed to always be working at his vision. He told me not to fret, that sometimes you have to earn a living. That made me feel better.)

I think too often our attention is on how to earn a living, or how to gain more experience, or how to use a new piece of equipment. We forget the enormous power of our medium. This is a shame, because the world's in trouble and needs our expertise. Not that we have all the answers, but we can join with experts and help them communicate their ideas and solutions to the world's problems. They need us. We need them. And the world needs the contribution from both of us.

I'm not suggesting that we all quit the jobs we enjoy and that put meals on the table, but I am suggesting that we find ways to do something more with our skills and hi-tech equipment.

ECO, Earth Communications Office in Los Angeles ([213] 277-1665) and Nashville, is a consortium of about 1000 motion picture and television professionals: actors, writers, directors, producers, lawyers and others who are finding ways to get the environmental message into their work. Lots of actors, like Tom Cruise, Olivia Newton John, Rosanne Cash, John Ritter, and scientists, such as the U.N.'s Dr. Noel Brown and The Smithsonian Institute's Dr. Thomas Lovejoy, are participating.

ECO's members have an impressive list of accomplishments. They've enlisted every major motion picture studio in Hollywood to start recycling

Producing to Make A Difference

programs. ECO members have produced and distributed public service TV spots to hundreds of television stations and movie theaters, organized major awareness events, and drawn together environmental experts to speak on water, energy, recycling, pollution, the ozone, deforestation, the Amazon rain forest ("Big Green"), and many other environmental topics. Script writers get the message into sit-coms and soap operas. Record stars are including fact sheets on their CD jackets about things people can do to save energy and water. They are also demanding that their record companies stop wasting resources by manufacturing oversized CD packaging. You don't have to join ECO to start thinking about environmental and social issues, but in a short time ECO presentations inspired me about what I could do to make a difference.

A single person can make a difference. And media producers–with access to millions of people–can effect even greater change.

I've consulted with a number of organizations and quite often their approach to media is quite weak. After all, they are concerned with issues, and they may not be as experienced with creating "television events" as Greenpeace or The Sierra Club. There are organizations that you can work with and would welcome your experience. There are probably several just waiting for you to call.

In cooperation with these organizations and their experts, you can use your production and organizational experience to help them deliver their message. You can ask for donations of time, equipment and materials and get it because a lot of people–who don't know what to do–are just waiting to be asked. You could write news releases or articles, produce PSAs, news segments, electronic press kits or even documentaries for local and/or national broadcast. You could create training programs. Or help experts prep for and get on television. There's no end to how your experience could benefit getting the message out there.

At the beginning of each year, I review my goals. This year I made a specific "work" goal to "do well by doing good." Besides getting involved with ECO, I found an opportunity to produce six PBS specials that will also have home video distribution. Not only are the shows assured of being broadcast but they are "how-to" programs which empower people with information that will improve both their lives and the environment. I couldn't be happier. Not since *Dolphin* have I found an opportunity to earn a livelihood and produce to make a difference all at the same time. It feels great.

These are little things you can do. There are big things you can do. It all counts. I encourage you to look at your life and your resources and find an opportunity where you can produce to make a difference. Now go get 'em!

FINANCING

WHERE DO YOU GET THE MONEY?

As I write this, I'm once again raising money. Will it ever end? No. Better get use to it folks, money-raising is part of producing. No money, no production. The more comfortable and skilled you can become with the process, the easier the money-raising will be.

Where do you get the money? Isn't this what we all want to know? With this column, I begin my one-on-one approach to financing, production and marketing solutions. My goal is to empower producers to develop opportunities and create successful strategies to get video programs made and marketed.

The most arduous of all steps is financing. And even money-raising cannot commence until a "package" is fully loaded with such items as script, talent, director, and business plan. Then the investor must be seduced with incentives and inspired. Video financing is like spinning plates in a circus. If the plates stop spinning, you lose your job. Financing is very creative, and no two deals are the same.

Home Video Companies

Private investment is not necessarily the most desirable form of financing. Private investors can't help you get their money back, since they have no business involvement in your program. Home video companies can. They have a financial stake in your program and will distribute it.

Home video companies should be one of the first shopping stops on your financial "hit list." The manufacturer sells your videos (through wholesalers) to video stores (for rental) and to mass merchants and bookstores (for sale). Naturally your program must have elements that are promotable and will appeal to a large audience. Otherwise you won't interest a large home video company that is looking to sell no fewer than 50,000 units per title. Most titles are movies. Only a hundred or so "specialty titles" sell in this range.

What you'll be looking for is an "advance against royalties," which you can use for production. A video company will want approval of the script and its realization. A common payment schedule would give the producer 25 percent upon signing an agreement, 25 percent upon principal videography, 25 percent upon rough-cut approval, and another 25 percent upon delivery.

The home video company will "recoup" its advance from the producer's royalty. Let's say the tape royalty is 20 percent of the wholesale gross receipts, and the tape is sold for $19.95 retail. With an approximate wholesale price average of $10, the producer will receive $2 per unit. If the producer was advanced $50,000, then the tape will have to sell 25,000 units to recoup its production advance. If the tape doesn't sell 25,000 units, then the producer will not see another dollar. The home video company will also ask to retain all other rights, such as television rights, which will help them protect their "downside." The good news is that the producer got the show made (and earned a production fee). The bad news is that all the upside potential of ancillary markets resides with the home video company. Whoever takes the financial risks, reaps the benefits. But what about financial arrangements that could leverage the financial "upside" more in the producer's favor?

The Educational or Business Market

Let's say that you had an idea from which two tapes could be created for two distinct markets through two different distributors. Consumer tapes priced below $29.95, and educational (or business) programs at $59, $99 or even $500. Both programs utilize the same source material, but you've found ways to "position" the material in two entirely different ways. For the home video version, you get a $50,000 advance. In your contract, you retain the "educational or business" version rights (as well as book and audio rights). For the educational version, you create a longer program and/or include a study guide or workbook to justify the higher price. You receive a second advance from the "educational distributor." Each program has a different title and is packaged distinctly.

Think about multiple markets, and you will expand both your revenue streams and communication opportunities. Also think "lines." It takes as much effort and money to market a series of tapes as it does a single program. And once you've found a market, why not sell them additional tapes? Create two or more tapes at the same time.

Let's suppose that the producer cannot raise enough money for the production from these distributors. Where does he or she go?

Private Investment

Many films and videos are financed by family, friends or business associates through limited partnerships. Each limited partner or investor puts up some money in exchange for a portion of the net profits. The traditional deal gives the limited partners or investors 50 percent of profits and the producer 50 percent. (The producer may share his or her 50 percent with talent, crew and others.) When the royalty checks start to come in, the investors are paid back their investment first. Sometimes they are paid an additional 15 to 30 percent before the 50/50 split. Sometimes the split is skewed in the favor of the investor, say 60/40. Sometimes investors are allowed to make back twice their investment then receive a small ongoing share of profits, say 10 to 25 percent. There are endless creative ways to cut the pie that compensate the investor for the risks they are taking.

If you privately fund a production <u>and</u> you've made a terrific program that many distributors want, you are in a much better position to leverage a better royalty deal and hold onto ancillary rights. This increases your upside if you have also made a reasonable deal with your investors.

Facilities as Partners

Why go through the hassle of raising money, however, if you can convince a facility with cameras, editing suites and videographics to be your business partner? Many facilities will be willing to engage in "soft dollar" financing. This works by the facility assuming "soft costs" (overhead, profit margin) and the producer paying "hard costs" (editor's time, tape stock, etc.). A facility may be willing to finance as much as 30 to 60 percent of your below-the-line expenses in exchange for an equity share (30 to 60 percent of the profits). Assume that the below-the-line budget (excluding producer, talent and writer's fees) is $100,000 and that a facility puts up $50,000 in services. You pay them $50,000 toward the hard costs. They may be entitled to a 50 percent profit participation (after you've received your deferred fees).

Or you may pay them back in full, give them a 10 or 20 percent "bump" (interest on their investment), as well as an equity position of 10-25 percent of profits. If you run out of time before the project is finished, you may have to beg more editing time rather than go back to your investors. Since the facility is your "partner," structure your deal so that everybody wins. Companies with postproduction and or duplication facilities are open to worthwhile projects. But again, these must be projects that truly will earn out in the marketplace, and your business and distribution plan must clearly show how this will be accomplished.

Next time we'll discuss other opportunities that can include other co-production partners, sponsors, television, premiums and other media forms. Feel free to be as creative in your thinking about how to finance your program as you are about your production design.

Now go get 'em!

SHAKING THE MONEY TREE

I continue to use each and every finance technique that I describe in this book. It pays to read and reread these ideas again and again. It will spark your imagination and help you with your own financing.

Have you been shaking that money tree? *Where Do You Get the Money* discussed deals with home video and non-theatrical (educational and business) distributors, private investors and facilities. This column deals with other co-production partners, sponsors, television, premiums and other media forms and the roles they may play in financing. You're going to have to be as creative in the way you put your deals together as you are in the way you produce your programs. Developing a taste for financial strategies will greatly influence your success.

Co-Ventures

Co-venturing is one of the best ways to finance your programs, because the risk is spread among other parties. An ideal co-venture might look something like this: an investor, a production company, and a distribution company each put up one third of the budget. The production company may put up fees or overhead, while the others put up cash. The normal distribution deal would allow the distributor to recoup its production advance in "first position" at the royalty rate (which is very slow) before giving the producer "overages" from which the producer and investor would recoup in "second position."

You can do better than this when you bring in two thirds of the financing. In the co-venture, everyone stands in the same position for recoupment and profit. In the one-third/one-third/one-third co-venture, the distribution company would receive and deduct a small distribution fee, duplication, marketing and advertising expenses from gross revenues. Then each partner would be paid back their investment at the same time. No one partner would stand in line before another, and all would share equally (one-third) in profits. What I like about this deal is that everyone has the same goals and is treated equally. Too frequently do producers and their investors stand last in line.

You also might go to television to raise financing. PBS, TBS, HBO, Showtime and many other cable (and network) systems need programming. They will either provide an advance, or pay upon broadcast for the television rights in your program. That still leaves all home video and other rights to exploit. While they may not cover the entire budget, they may supply a significant portion of your financing. Some systems, like HBO, are putting up a few million for small made-for-movies, but retaining all rights. The question before a producer is "do you want to get it done?" or "do you want to try to retain some rights for 'upside' profits?" Most just opt to get their programs and videos made because they feel financing is scarce, but it doesn't have to be this way.

Premiums

Like their cousins, the personalized coffee mug and baseball hat, videos have entered the premium market. Why? First, they have a very high perceived value. Consumers know videos cost $19.95 or more. If they can get one free-with-a-purchase, or as a low-cost purchase-with-a-purchase, they feel it's a great deal. Many advertisers and their clients have been using videos to draw in new consumers for their products, because video can deliver a very targeted demographic. Burger King's video promotion using *Teenage Mutant Ninja Turtles* sold well over 10 million units. With new videos coming out every few weeks, kids and their families develop a Whopper habit–which is the real goal of this premium or incentive program.

These big premium deals are few and far between for most producers. There are, however, many companies that would buy 5000 or 10,000 or even 100,000 videos if they felt it would expand the market for their core product. A premium deal in the bag can help finance your program. How does this work? Say you are making a one-hour how-to program. You make a deal with a company that you will cut a "special version" (half hour) of the program for them. It will have special packaging and a promotional spot on the tape. They pay you $1 (it could be a tad more or less) over cost for 50,000 units. That's $50,000 you can put into the production. They have a premium, and you have some financing. You own the sole rights to the long version for the video markets. Everyone wins.

Sponsors

Producers everywhere look to sponsorship as a means to finance video, but most miss the point. Unwittingly, they pitch sponsors to put up production money. Wrong! Not that important! Producers say, "Wiese, are you crazy?" and I say "No." Producers aren't thinking of the big picture. Why get only $25,000, or $50,000 toward your production budget when you can get millions in advertising and cross-promotion? And it's much easier to get a "yes" out of sponsors.

First, realize that sponsors have their own agendas. They are trying to sell their services and products. Unless your video can help them do that, they won't be interested. If they are interested, go for cross-promotion. Say you want to produce a series of children's tapes. The sponsor wants to introduce a new product to kids so the kids will use the product early in their lives and develop a loyalty to it. Why not have the sponsor commit to promoting your video in their next multi-million dollar print and television campaign? (And you can also sell them premiums.)

Shaking the Money Tree

Such a campaign would have built enormous public awareness about your children's video–far more than the paltry $75,000 that most video companies would spend on video marketing for your program. With that awareness, you should be able to strike a much better advance deal with a video distributor once the sponsor's promotion ends. And consumers who didn't get the video through the sponsor's promotion may buy it.

Sponsored Financing with a Twist

Last year I produced a comedic Monopoly-like board game called *Goin' Hollywood*, in which the players are producers trying to get their movies made "any way they can." The game was launched regionally in Los Angeles. We were actually involved in two businesses. The first was selling board games through WaldenBooks and gift stores. The second was selling advertising. Since we had many "power spots" (famous locations and businesses) on the board, we sold "ad space" for them to such places as Mondrian, L'Ermitage and Chateau Marmont, and to magazines such as *Premiere*, *Variety* and *Hollywood Reporter*. Rather than take money which we certainly needed, we learned we could get much more value out of our "ad sale" by taking free hotel rooms and catering at the hotels where we held our "game playing" press parties, and by bartering for full-page color ads in the magazines.

Press parties and ads were expenses we would have incurred anyway. By bartering the ads, we accomplished much more. (Since the real cost of the hotel rooms and ad space was less to the sponsors, we were able to barter much easier that if we were looking for cash.)

These are only a few of the kinds of creative financing, bartering and cross-promotion that you need to think about as you pull all the elements together for your video programs. Every time you find a creative way to finance, it may lower your risk, improve your marketing opportunities, and increase revenues. Now go get 'em.

WHAT INVESTORS WANT

Producers should cultivate the art of listening. There are many things an investor may want (in addition to financial return). If you can really hear, and learn what these things are, it will be easier for you to reach your goal.

When I first started raising money for documentaries, I was very surprised by what some investors wanted. It had little or nothing to do with their investment–they really didn't care whether their money was returned or not. They were interested in what the film had to say and in getting a message out. Some were just interested in participating with filmmakers.

Unsophisticated investors (meaning those that haven't invested in films or videos before) go through your prospectus, listen to your presentation, and scrutinize you very carefully. They ask many questions that you must be prepared to answer. They certainly will have questions that you will need to answer. Many questions will go unasked but are very important to address during your presentation.

Here are some things investors like and need to hear:

1.   The video will make a lot of money, more than their investment, and maybe a whole lot more than that. (How can you demonstrate this? Will it be sold to the corporate market? To the consumer market? By direct mail or through direct response ads? How many will be sold and at what price? Over what period?

2.   There will be a large publicity campaign that will generate enormous public excitement and awareness, and lots of people will want to see the video they've been hearing about. (How can you demonstrate this? Is there a hook that suddenly interests a large segment of the population? Today that might be something about police violence or on a patriotic subject. Before you make your video, you must think about publicity which will help the video find greater distribution.)

3.   Your video is a class act with high profile elements. There are well-known, prestigious stars, directors and/or writers in your video. (Is your video based on a best-selling book, a life story, a high profile news event, a literary masterpiece, or a corporate training breakthrough? What makes your video stand head and shoulders among the competition?)

4.   Your video will be shot in exquisite locations, or will be loaded with special effects, or will have some visual element that is really terrific, or all of the above. (Do you have footage of that great volcanic eruption, or whale footage, or great spaceship fly-bys?)

5.   They can participate or get involved at some level. Can they visit the set, go to parties, go to the premiere, meet the actors? (What can you offer that gives your investors some participation but doesn't crimp what you have to do during production?)

6.   They have a choice about investing in your video or not investing in it. They don't want to be pressured, or coerced, or sense that the video's existence depends on their money. They do not want to feel that without their money the video won't get made. This puts too much responsibility on the investors. It's the producer's job to get the video made.

Some Other Thoughts

1. Money attracts money.

If you already have some money in your pocket (especially your own), it will bring a sigh of relief to your investors. No one wants to be first (unless there is some financial reward for doing so). By sharing the risk with other investors, everyone's comfort level rises.

If you have done your homework and put together an admirable package and an honest agreement, you will find investors. If your project has integrity and if you are offering a fair deal to investors, you already have an advantage over other producers beating on the same doors. Honesty is very attractive to investors, who know it when they see it.

2. Don't confuse money with quality.

There will be lots of videos that look better than yours because they have bigger budgets, but that doesn't mean they are better. Investors recognize that good videos can be made about powerful subjects on smaller budgets.

A good video is competitive in the marketplace because audiences for good videos are growing. The number of video festivals in this country boggles the imagination. There are VCRs in over 70 percent of all homes. People use video in business. They watch video for entertainment. Schools use video for education. Tastes are changing, movie audiences are getting older, and they are demanding more from movies. Audiences often turn to video during their leisure and work hours. They want better, more intelligent material, and videos that bring meaning, knowledge or new skills to their lives.

Independents have one significant advantage over networks and large video companies: they can make goods videos for little money. This is attractive to investors because there is tremendous upside in producing quality videos for reasonable budgets. Independents know that the limited money they are able to raise must go into the video and be seen on the screen. The fewer fees taken out of the budget, the better the investment package appears to investors. No investor wants to fall victim to a "hit and run" producer. If you make quality videos, you will attract quality investors.

3. When you want a hundred people to show up at a party you invite a hundred and thirty.

When you line up your investors, you overbook because some may fall through and not deliver on their pledges. Some will have "cash flow" or "stock market" or "personal" problems when it's time for you to pick up their check. If you have commitments for more money than you actually need, it does wonders for your self esteem. That attitude attracts even more investors. People run to abundance and run from scarcity. If you have more money than you need, you have leverage in your distribution negotiations. You won't have to cave in on deal points. If you don't have all the money you need, the money does the talking and you lose some of your negotiating strength. If you don't need the money you can make tougher deals, which benefits your investors.

4. A money raising technique:

Whether investors say "yes" or "no" to your project, be sure to get other names and contacts from them. If they say "yes," they'll be inclined to think of others who might like to invest. If they say "no," they may feel guilty and at least will want to give you something for free–like someone else's name. Fine. You can use every contact you can get.

5. Make sure your lawyer complies with all state laws and SEC regulations in preparing your investment documents.

If you proceed in an unprofessional, haphazard manner, you can be shut down and suffer terrible consequences. For example, you are not allowed to advertise your project in newspapers or magazines. In some cases you must qualify your investors–they must be able to afford the risk–and they may be required to have earned over $250,000 per year for the last several years. Discuss this with your attorney to learn whether he or she must screen and qualify every potential investor.

Summary

It baffles the brain to understand what investors want. I continue to be surprised. The main point is to get out there and talk about your project. Your enthusiasm is a greater magnet for finding investors than your idea. (Really!) It's not only about money, it's about doing good work, making a difference, and sharing knowledge. Frequently, some of the higher human aspirations will emerge in the form of investors. And no sense being shy about asking for money–you don't get weird when you ask for videotape stock. It's simply another resource. Money is more abundant than you think. Now go get ',em!

INVESTORS, WHERE ART THEE? PART I

You're in a jungle. You hear sounds from every direction. You see evidence of animals being here, but you don't see them. Investors are like that. Everywhere we go, we see the results of money being spent. Where does this money came from? Your job is to find the investor. It's a jungle out there.

More than the latest chip camera, more than the new hi-def monitor, more than the beta version of a graphics program, producers want to know how to raise money for their projects. The next few columns are designed to help producers in their search for the illusive grail: financing.

The first step is not getting the money, but preparing a package, a pre-production presentation that outlines the project, cast, budget, schedule and distribution as well as a marketing plan that predicts anticipated returns. This requires that the producer be good at writing, designing and packaging the video project, be enthusiastic, be thick-skinned enough for the numerous rejections he or she will encounter, have some experience in financing (or have partners who are), and some idea about where the money is and how to go about getting it.

Private Investment

Going to private investors is clearly the most expedient method for funding video productions if the projects have the ability to return the investment (and hopefully some profit.) Private investment allows you much more freedom to get your video made because <u>anyone with money can help you.</u> Distribution, however, may still be a problem, and investors will have to be convinced that distribution will be forthcoming.

Confidence

Winning over investors requires confidence and integrity. For many, this confidence comes only after they have prepared a strong package, a fabulous idea, a strong script, a great crew, superb actors, a savvy lawyer and accountant, and a distributor with experienced marketing skills. This confidence inspires confidence in others and is a critical requirement regardless of where you are looking for financial support.

The producer also instills confidence in other participants. Everyone is confident that the project is a good idea and therefore will commit to it. At precisely the right moment (not too early and not too soon) when the alchemical cauldron begins to heat up and the package is finally ready, the producer goes out into the market place to secure the final ingredient: the money.

71

The right moment arrives when a producer can say with certainty to an investor, "It's happening. The train is moving down the tracks. Do you want to get aboard?" He gives the investor a choice of investing. The producer makes it clear that everyone is committed to the project, that investment is really not a problem (even though it is, or the producer wouldn't still be talking to investors), and that the investor is free to not invest. In the heat of the excitement, many investors surrender to the moment. The producer must then quickly close the deal.

Many producers make the mistake of saying "help" and looking to the investor to make it all happen. "I need you to invest, otherwise it may not happen." No investor wants to be in this position. He wants to feel secure, and what better way to give him this feeling than by not really needing his money.

Critical Mass

If you assemble your pre-production package, slowly and carefully, you can achieve a critical mass that will improve your odds. "Critical mass" means you build the elements to leverage other elements. If you're a new producer, it may be more difficult to get the big star first. So you get the script or video idea that begets a strong director that begets a big star. Start where you can succeed best, and build from there. If you can get the big star first, that helps you leverage a director and financing. The more successful you are every step of the way, the more confident you feel, and the better equipped you are to go to the next stage. Producing is a process of taking lots of small focused steps so at the end of your journey you have a complete video.

Keep your focus and goal clearly in front of you. Having the intelligence to separate your goals from distractions is basic. Continuing to take the right steps in an efficient and effective manner is the day-to-day work that must be done. You must have a realistic idea of how and where to start (appropriate to your station in life and what you can really do) and accurately assess you ability to inspire others. This focus and the sense that you will accomplish your goal elicits more support and agreement than anything. People want to believe, they want to be led, and they want you to be the one to bring it all together.

With a prepared package and your newfound confidence, it's time to start pitching. But not everyone is marching to the same drummer. Different people will be moved and influenced in different ways.

Right-and Left-Brain Pitches

It's important to know who your audience is when you are pitching your project, and to tailor your pitch to his or her perception. Although it's never as simplistic as what I'm about to describe, this may give you some useful ideas.

Let's assume that there are basically two types of people in the world; each perceives the world very differently from the other. One type primarily uses their right brain, the other their left. (Actually, most people shift back and forth between both parts of their brains, but let me continue.) Here are some examples of these two kinds of people you will encounter during your production.

Right-Brain People

Your <u>actor</u> is interested in the <u>emotions</u> of the character he or she is to play. Your <u>director</u> is interested in a compelling idea and the best way to <u>visualize</u> it. Your right-brained <u>investor</u> responds to the emotions, feel, look, and textural quality of your video idea.

Left-Brain People

Your <u>banker</u> is interested in analyzing your contracts and the concrete ways in which the loan will be repaid.

Your <u>left-brained investor</u> wants to know <u>how quickly</u> his or her money will be returned, and <u>how much profit</u> the video is likely to generate over <u>what period of time.</u>

In talking with your actors, the director and the composer, you will usually use evocative language because this is the mode that best suits their perceptions. You paint a picture with your words. You describe the vision for the video, its mood and tone.

When you are looking for investors, you may have to radically shift gears. Your banker and investors are not terribly keen on the mood and tone of your video. That's not what they want to hear. They want just the facts. Schedules, cash flow charts, spread sheets, market shares and bottom lines. The very stuff that drives artistic people crazy are what they rely on in order to evaluate your project.

Different people perceive the world differently. If you want to communicate successfully with these different people, you need to understand how they perceive the world, and tailor your presentation appropriately. People perceive the world in a variety of primary modes, and frequently switch between modes: kinetic, acoustic, visual, etc. Successful communicators are aware of the modes their audience is accessing. Successful producers are aware of the modes of perception of their investors and pitch accordingly.

Videographers understand their audiences modes very well and can lead them by their senses through a video experience. Clearly, this is a valuable area that requires further thought and investigation.

About Investing

Many investors will be in their left brains when they are thinking about the use of their money. One great problem with the business of raising money is that you really can't, with any sense of certainty, show your investor how and when this money will be returned. Profit is an unknown. "Well, it depends on so very many things..." is not what your investor or banker wants to hear. It makes him or her real nervous.

Our business is very, very speculative, and the outcome is beyond the producer's control. How does he or she know that the video will receive the right marketing campaign? Will the video be released at the right time? Will we get an honest count from our distributor? Most investors have heard about, or worse yet, gotten burned from a movie or video deal gone bad. No wonder investors seem scarce.

Delicate Bubble of Belief

So what do most producers do? They block such horrible thoughts from their minds to protect the sanctity of their investor's tranquillity and confidence. Besides, it's far more enjoyable for the producer to use his or her story-telling skills to talk about "this wonderful video we are making." The investor is warmed from the producer's enthusiastic glow, and it's hard to "just say no." If the investor looked too deeply into what could go wrong, it could be depressing and might convince him to do something else with his money. It's better for the producer to focus on the world of possibilities and happy endings.

So the dance between producer and investor begins. There are unspoken rules to be observed so that the delicate bubble of belief is not broken. The producer's job is to enthusiastically sustain the vision for what is to be. Like a magician, he keeps everyone believing. His vision is a dream that he's trying to make come true through the efforts of others. "If we just keep working, and you just keep investing, we can do miraculous things!" The more people the producer has lined up, the more real it begins to look to everyone, and the more real the vision actually becomes. The producer's art is a kind of alchemy. He mixes in enthusiasm, talent and money, and voilaa! A video cassette comes out of the smoke. Now go get 'em.

INVESTORS, WHERE ART THEE? PART II

Like Ulysses, the producer's quest for financing leads him into mysterious territory, unknown landscapes, and into the domiciles of strange creatures.

Sometimes, however, the search involves waiting, and in some mysterious way investors are drawn to you. Imagine financing your video without ever leaving home.

Four times this kind of strange thing happened to me. I've been packaging a television and home video series about spiritual masters, which includes such extraordinary people as The Dalai Lama of Tibet, and other Eastern and Western teachers who address contemporary issues. The series explores how to live a spiritual life in the modern world. This, I believe, is a very difficult project to fund because the opportunity for huge paybacks are small unless of course we have a surprise blockbuster. But financial rewards are not what this particular project is about, and perhaps that's what people are responding to when they want to contribute.

Serendipity Reigns

Out of the blue (I love that phrase) came two calls. People had money they wanted to invest in film and video. "Did I have any ideas?" The first caller was looking for other kinds of investments besides real estate. I told him about a few commercial projects and then sheepishly about *Masters Among Us*, a spiritual masters series. This one took hold. Rather than invest, he offered to go out and find corporate contributions. Today, he faxed me a redraft of our proposal that he thought would be helpful. A former theology student and successful businessman, he was looking for something else to do. He found it.

Call number two was from another man looking for interesting opportunities. Besides real estate, he had bought a high-end video camera and has partnered with a top news cameraman. The spiritual masters project interested him as an investment with the possible caveat that we hire his crew for some of the shoots.

Then I received an unsolicited call from a former investor. Every year I send him a royalty check from *Dolphin*, a film I made 12 years ago. He told me that he just ran across a check I'd written in 1986 behind a drawer and "would I write him another one?" Certainly. When he asked me what I was up to, I told him about spiritual masters and the Dalai Lama who had agreed to participate. He told me that he is now on the board of directors of a foundation that gives money to spiritual media and the arts, and that I should apply for a grant!

And lastly, a friend of mine was talking to a friend about our project. She surprised him by saying she'd like to invest a very large sum (when another investment pays off). I've been in this business long enough to be skeptical until the check is in the bank. But the point I'm trying to illustrate is that something else seems to be happening. None of these financing sources were solicited. They just happened!

My sense is that strong intention ("this project is going to happen") combined with serendipity ("how I don't know exactly") and a lot of hard work are the ingredients of this success.

Every week we refine and strengthen our presentation package. With every new contact, spiritual master or crew member, investor or contributor, video, television or audio deal, we strengthen our ability to get the project made. People feel this, and want to be a part of it.

Even if you believe that there's a little magic happening here, you can't stay in bed and wish it to happen. You have to do the conventional things to find financing. I contact former investors, ferret our new possibilities, look for facilities deals and distribution and marketing opportunities. Still, there is this nagging feeling that there is another level on which this project is coming together. There have just been to many serendipitous occurrences.

Time Allocation

I have become more conscious of my time. I only have a limited amount, and I want to use it well and make it count. I don't like to spend time developing projects, unless I am confident (and committed) that they will get made. I certainly don't like to try to raise money where the chances of getting "no's" are high. I want results.

The Three-Strike Rule

I've developed and produced enough home video projects to know where to go to find financing and distribution. Over the last few years, I have developed what I call my "three-strike rule." After three, unsuccessful pitches to video distributors, I move on. Three rejections (by qualified buyers) means the marketplace is telling me "no thanks." I figure I should know who is most likely to buy the project. Of course, you have to pick your three pitches very carefully. You don't pitch a spiritual masters project to an exploitation distributor. (However, given my recent experience, this may not be such a bad idea!)

Videos have a shorter gestation rate than films. I like that. They are quicker to develop, cost far less to produce, and are released into the marketplace months later. The financing arc on a feature may take years; with a video, it's only months. If you like instant gratification, videos will suit you.

At any one time, I have a dozen videos (or TV programs) in development, a handful in production, and many more in release. Features move forward very slowly (or not at all), although the financial rewards and visibility are much greater.

What Flavor Investor?

There are two kinds of investors. One is unsophisticated in the video business; the other, may be a video distributor who knows the video business inside and out. Which is better? Who do you go for first? If financing is your goal and you feel capital is scarce, then you take what you can get from either type of investor.

Conventional wisdom suggests it's more advantageous to get financing from an end user, like a broadcaster or home video company. The thinking goes that if the end user invests in a video, he or she is motivated and capable of getting the money back by making sure the video is successfully distributed. The power of self-interest is not to be underestimated. If your financing doesn't come from an end user, you must rely on other resources.

A second argument frequently made for going to end users for financing is that it's usually easier. An end user understands video deals. It doesn't matter if your end-user investment partner is domestic or foreign, because he or she will protect their own downside–either through their own distribution efforts or by selling it to others.

The other school of thought suggests that nonvideo-industry financing, or the private investor route, is best. This type of investor is less sophisticated and makes fewer demands about the kind of video produced.

Many, many videos have been financed by private investors. Now, however, some savvy investors are staying away from videos because they know the marketplace is flooded and easy profits are harder to come by. Today the competition to sell to the video rental market is greater. A retailer no longer buys most B titles, but prefers As which are feature films almost solely produced by the studios. Video rental stores don't want to stock hard-to-market B films and videos when they can have A pictures (for the same price) that bring greater visibility and higher rentals. For an investor in independent B videos today, the risk is heightened, and the rate of return diminished. Why shouldn't he/she look for other kinds of investments?

Nevertheless, making a financial killing is not necessarily the motivating factor for some investors. My *Videography* column, *What Investors Want*, explores what will motivate your potential investors. Until next time, don't go get 'em, let 'em come to you.

HOW DO YOU MAKE THE MONEY BACK?

I can't say it enough–you have to understand distribution agreements inside and out. Be sure you understand how the money will come back to you (and your investors). You have to be absolutely clear about this, or you and all your partners are in deep trouble.

Ah, distribution... the word sends producers running in fear and/or loathing. Unfortunately, many of them don't really want to face distribution, and they dive into production only to face it when they surface for air.

What's so bad about distribution, and why does it get such a bad rap? The experience of many producers is that distribution revenues fall short of expectations projected in the business plan. Informing investors of this fact is always unpleasant.

Recently, I've given a lot of thought to this whole issue, because–like all producers–I think there's got to be a better way. I'd like to set up a home video distribution label, so I won't have to go hat in hand to distributors every time I have a program I want to produce.

I've worn the producer's hat, the distributor's hat, and many hats in between. I have these recurring dreams of hundreds of smiling investors raving over my last video, patting me on the back, and filling my hands with wads of money for my next project. Then I wake up.

Why can't this dream be real? The context in which our business exists goes something like this: "We all know there is the 'business' part of show business. It's tough, ugly and full of cheats. You can't blame me for wanting mine now, can you?" All negotiations seem to end with "I get mine now, thank you." High paid lawyers structure deals that only nuclear physicists can understand. Everyone (the distributor, the investor, the producer, and the star) wants to stand first in line for profits (if any). Since everybody knows that there never are any profits, they want a big fee now. Hence, ridiculously large budgets.

Financing and distribution deals are definitely not about setting up win-win situations. "Somebody's got to win, somebody's got to lose" is Hollywood's distribution theme song. We need distribution deal structures that benefit distributors and producers and their investors. How hard could that be?

Distributors have convinced producers that without them producers don't stand a chance. Even if you leave the office for the next distributor, the deal you're offered is essentially the same. I don't care whether it's a royalty deal, a distribution fee deal, or a joint venture, when you run the numbers the basic video distribution deal is 80/20. That's 80 percent for the distributor and 20 (or less) for the producer. The distributor makes a profit long before the producer (and the investors). Why? "Why not?" responds the distributor. "Without distribution, you'd be nowhere." Only hit-making producers have been able to retort, "Hey, without my program, you'd have zip to distribute!" But most don't have this clout.

Suppose, however, that producers everywhere woke up one morning, and the entire context of the business had shifted. Let's imagine that The Creation of the Product is everything, and producers began saying "Listen up Mr. Distributor, without our programs there'd be no distribution business." By making the product supreme, all deals become subservient to the creators, the producers and their investors. Those who contribute to the creation of The Product–be it money, creative services, a script or other elements–are the real benefactors at Gross Receipt Time.

Well, that's not really going to happen in our lifetime, but here's a deal structure that does make sense. Suppose investors, producers and distributors came to the table, and all agreed that what each of them contributed had pretty much an equal value. And let's further suppose that each partner (the distribution company, an investor, and the production company) agreed to put up one third of the budget.

The distributor agrees to pay for manufacturing and packaging the cassettes and for marketing. The distributor's money would be recouped first. And because the distributor is providing a very real service and is risking additional monies on manufacturing and marketing, he is entitled to receive an equitable distribution fee (say 15 percent). Thereafter, the actual marketing and distribution costs are deducted, and all the three partners share equally in thirds.

What I particularly like about this structure is that everyone has the same goal. Everyone stands under the waterfall. Since everyone's goal is the same, everyone receives equal treatment. There is no preferred standing.

Let's run the numbers between both deal structures. We'll first look at a traditional deal.

Twenty Percent Royalty Deal   (50,000 Units Sold)

Price of tape: $ 19.95 Retail
                    $ 11.37 Wholesale

Producer's royalty: $ 2.27 (20 Percent)

Gross receipts: $ 568,500 (received by distributor)

Minus:
Producer's royalty: -113,700 ($100,000 Production budget plus $13,700 in royalty
                                 overages [to share with investors])

Duplication costs: -112,500 ($2.25 Per tape)

Marketing costs: - 75,000 ($1.50 Per tape x 50,000 units)

Net to distributor: $267,300 (Effective 47 percent fee)

What's happened with this standard structuring is that even with successful sales of 50,000 units the producer only makes $13,500 above and beyond the production costs. If he's raised the money through a 50/50 limited partnership the investors get paid back their $100,000 investment (the budget). Then the producer and investor split $13,500. Each gets $6,250. Big deal.

But look what wealth rains on the distributor. He pays duplication and marketing costs and nets $267,500. Yes, the distributor has overhead, sales staff to pay, and rent - but he still comes out way ahead of the producer and the investors, who've had their money at risk for a very long time.

The "Thirds" Partnership Deal (50,000 Units Sold)

Price of tape: $ 19.95 Retail
                    $ 11.37 Wholesale

Gross receipts: $568,500

Minus:
15 percent distributor's fee
                    - 85,275

Duplication costs   -112,500   ($2.25 Per tape)
Marketing costs   - 75,000   ($1.50 Per tape)
Production budget -100,000
Net to partners: $ 195,725
Each partner: $ 65,241

If each party puts up $33,333 (a third of the production budget), then each one nearly doubles their investment. <u>And they do so all at the same time</u>. Meanwhile, the distributor is still rewarded with $85,000 as a fee for the distribution service, which can be applied to overhead and yield a profit.

I'm a producer. I value the product that my investors have allowed me to make. I'd like to see them recoup their investment, and then some. With a win-win deal, everyone gets results. And when the investor wins, there is every likelihood that they will invest again. When I set up my distribution company, I'll let you know. Until then, go get 'em.

The Chicken Or The Egg: Financing Issues

You're making a painting. You start with a sketch, an outline. You add some general colors, and you begin to add definition. Finally, you do the details, the highlights. The truth is <u>you really start everywhere at once</u> because you have to see the finished product in your mind's eye before you even start.

Producers are confused about where to start. "Do I look for distribution first? Or do I look for financing?" You look for both simultaneously.

I am currently putting together a series of six one-hour programs for television and home video. This documentary series is best suited for PBS broadcast, and then will be packaged as a six-part set for home video. The series will be promoted as an "event" with a book, audio and home video release, all timed day-and-date with the television broadcast. There is foreign sales potential as well. (This model is akin to *The Civil War*, the recent series that was literally a multi-media event, with simultaneous home video, book and broadcast release dates.)

Production financing for such a project comes from many sources. Here's how you start.

The Value of A Good Name

The first step is lining up "name" actors (recognized men and women that have some popularity with viewing audiences), because obtaining distribution is critical. Name actors are what will interest home video distributors. In turn, their sales to the home video buyers will be easier with recognizable names. Most consumers will hear or read about the programs (before they actually see them), and names will entice them to tune in or purchase the video, book or audio. So the first thing to do is secure name talent.

Not so easy. Because without financing or distribution in place, why would actors (or their agent) even want to talk until a "serious" offer can be made? Normally they wouldn't unless: (1) they believed in the project (and they do), and this is where quality helps; and (2) we had a track record, and they believed that we'd be able to pull it off (they do). No star wants to lend their name to a project that may not succeed. Talent puts you into a position to get "serious" with distributors and investors.

The Relationship Between Broadcast and Home Video

A broadcaster is very important because PBS exposure, for example, is a kind of "theatrical release" for a home video. A nationwide broadcast can capture enormous publicity, which in turn sells video cassettes. While we may not be able to count on PBS for cash (they take years to find sponsors

83

to underwrite programming), we may be able to get a broadcast date if the series was offered to PBS at a very low price. (Start to see how all this fits together?)

Okay, now a brief recap. Stars are interested in the project, but not signed. PBS is interested in the stars and the project. Several home video companies are ready to negotiate. This brings us to the Book Deal and the Audio Deal.

Book Deal

Our book agent tells us that he knows three or four publishers who are willing to give us an advance on a companion book to the series. These advances range from very large amounts to very small sums and are based on whether PBS airs the show locally or nationally.

Audio Deal

The same thing goes for the audio cassette deal. The audio company, however, believes that the talent involved is the main driving force for audio sales. They like the possibility that a companion book may be published, because a book's penetration into stores may help to leverage an audio cassette with the same title. Audio is a small piece of the financing pie, but every little bit helps.

Pay and Basic Cable

We are also approaching the cable networks. If they give us a license fee for the program, it may take up any shortfall from the home video company. Then we could forgo a PBS broadcast. And even if the series airs less on cable than on PBS and reduces public awareness, the objective is to get the series. This is another possible scenario.

Foreign Sales

There are some foreign television and home video sales to be made with the series, if according to our foreign sales rep the names are recognizable internationally. These names will also have to work in the U.S., which is the primary market for the program. Foreign pre-sales (to home video and television) may make up as much as 40 percent of the financing.

Time for another recap. Each market represents a possible piece of the financing puzzle. Everyone is interested, but won't commit until the others do. It's a matter of getting everyone ready to say "yes" then closing all the deals at the same time. Broadcast and home video distribution deals will lock the stars.

Investors

Distribution and broadcast deals will bring in financing, because they will provide comfort to any investors if we still need their money to cover production cost. With distribution in place, investors can be approached. Their involvement will be predicated on the question, "Who's distributing the program?" It's unrealistic to expect anyone to invest until that question is answered. It's most likely that investor money is going to come after distribution is in place at the tail end of the financing maze. (Most producers unknowingly begin looking for investors. It's very, very difficult to close deals for the reasons just mentioned.)

If, however, we sell off all the rights (home video, pay TV, all foreign rights), there may not be any upside (positive reason) for an investor. That is if we receive advances for these rights in order to finance the series, that may be the only money we (and the investor) will ever see unless the series is a big hit. That's a risky proposition and may not offer enough upside for an investor. The ideal situation is to sell as few rights as possible to raise production financing (and assure distribution), but not so much that there's no upside left for an investor.

One way to piece it all together is to selectively sell off territories. Pre-sell U.S. to home video and television, and then pre-sell foreign rights in England, Japan or France. Then take in investors. The upside for the investors are the unsold territories, such as Italy, Spain, Germany, Australia and a number of other key territories. The investors will look to those territories (and overages, if any) as their primary source of recoupment.

Contributions

There are also people who may want to support the series with a non-profit donation. Some people like the content and inherent message in a series. In order to take in non-profit contributions, we have to financially structure the series as a non-commercial project. (What that means is that we can't have any investors. The minute we accept non-profit money, we can't also have "profit participation" for investors. It's one or the other. Although some producers have played it both ways, we won't. Get your lawyer's opinion on this matter before proceeding.) We sometimes receive individuals' funds indirectly through a non-profit organization. The contributor gets a tax benefit and writes a check to the non-profit foundation, which deducts a five percent administration fee and then writes a check to us.

Summary

A lot is involved but if you know the true potential of your project and understand what elements leverage other elements, you can save a lot of time. You put your effort in those areas that will produce the greatest result. You identify the players and understand their motivations for either licensing, advancing, pre-buying or investing in your program. We're still in the midst of putting this one together, and significant progress has been made in a few short weeks. I'll let you know when it's in the bag. Until then, now you go get 'em.

MARKETING

INFOMERCIALS: WHERE'S THE INFO?

Infomercials really have one purpose: to sell product. They may do this by entertaining and informing, but ultimately there's a "call to action." Orders must be taken, or you're out of business. Give the audience info during the infomercial, but leave them with the sense that there is more to be learned by purchasing your "product"–which may be videos, audios or books. Then deliver products loaded with information adding to their knowledge.

I said I'd never work in television, never work in New York (or Los Angeles), and never do an infomercial. Never say never. It doesn't work.

But why infomercials? I hate infomercials. I don't watch infomercials. I'd never order anything from an infomercial. I don't trust them. I think they are manipulative. They are snake-oil's first cousin. I don't like 'em. But I have a vision....

I love special-interest videos. I've developed, produced, marketed and consulted on 300 or more home videos. Children's, music videos, comedies, documentaries, how-to's and genres that haven't even been named yet. They're great. Unlike movies, you can produce them quickly. Five months, six months–boom, they're done and out in the world!

But here's the rub. Video stores don't care about special-interest videos. They want movies. Well, maybe if it's a Jane Fonda video or a Shirley MacLaine video, they'll buy hundreds of thousands. But usually not. To sell special interest videos through retail stores, you have to first sell the wholesaler who has to sell the retailer who has to sell the customer who is a very busy and distracted creature and will, at best, only give you a few seconds of his or her time. It's tough. Real tough.

Infomercials, however, are a perfect medium to preview original programs. The viewer is clicking around the dial and–Whammo–something interesting appears. What is it? An infomercial. Let's watch. Your video product is pumped directly into someone's living room. No layers of middlemen. As a producer, marketer and video publisher of original, special interest programs, infomercials have great potential.

Last year I developed and produced a series of television/video programs for Los Angeles PBS station KCET called Lifeguides. These are empowering videos for the professional and the individual. They were made available through 1-800 numbers following the shows. And they were sold during PBS' pledge nights, through direct mail, and through retail outlets. One of the shows really took off. *Diet For A New America*, based on the Pulitzer-nominated book by John Robbins, made some chilling connections between our animal-based diet and degenerative diseases (cancer, strokes, heart attacks, diabetes, etc.) and the environment. Everyone I've talked to changed their diet after watching the show, and many people bought multiple copies of the program to give to their friends ("call 1-800-765-7890"). The video received the Genesis Award for "Outstanding TV Documentary on PBS" and has become an advocacy piece for vegetarian, environmental, and animal rights groups. This is what I want to do with videos! But, it's real tough, as those of you who have produced social documentaries well understand.

Mission Statement

It's a new year. I wrote a mission statement for 1992. I've found it enormously helpful in managing my work. Besides eliminating the day-to-day distractions, a mission statement becomes my value-filter through which I can judge my priorities. I try to spend most of my time taking steps toward my goals. It also has the added benefit of attracting worthwhile projects. Try writing one, and see for yourself.

Here's mine:

> *"Our mission is to empower and improve the quality of human life and the environment by creating worthwhile and educational communication tools."*

So, it made sense to look to the infomercial–the perfect preview medium–to try to display and sell the kinds of videos alluded to in my mission statement. Shortly after having this notion and writing my mission statement, I was contracted to produce a series of health-oriented infomercials (the product, a bundle of videos, audios and books.) Each infomercial is based on the work of health professionals.

Here's some of what I learned:

- You need a concept that's memorable. ("The Juiceman," "Hooked-On-Phonics," "Where There's A Will There's An A.")

- You need an appealing, charismatic personality who either introduces the product or who has created the product. (Jane Fonda, Kathy Smith)

- Testimonials by celebrities seem to be important, especially if the celebrity says they are not getting paid to tout the product (e.g. Martin Sheen in Tony Robbins' infomercial.)

- Testimonials by real people are great. Use enough people, and there will be somebody to relate to for every type of viewer in your audience.

- Credibility is very important to overcome people's fears about the product, about ordering from television, about getting their money back, etc.

- The product must be simple and easy to understand.

- Americans want quick results. The product must offer quick results. "Thin thighs in 30 days" is a promise too good to be true. Sign me up.

The basic structure of an infomercial is:

- Grabber–An emotional, personal element that gets attention.

- Problem–An undeniable, horrible problem.

- Product–Here's what will bring relief, deliver results, make you richer, sexier, or healthier.

- Solution–How you too can change. The benefits.

- Close–Why and How to buy, incentives, the cost.

- Guarantee–If you're not satisfied... money-back guarantee.

Concepts and rules I don't buy:

- It's better if you can't find it in stores. (Sometimes people see an appliance or product in an infomercial, and don't order it. But the first time they see something similar in a retail store, they buy it there.)

- You have to appeal to greed (real estate courses) and vanity (cosmetics, hair restoration products). These are lesser human qualities. I'd like to appeal to higher desires such as education, better health, improving relationships, etc. Ultimately people realize that more stuff won't make them better, happier people.

- Don't let your customer get away. Keep the 1-800 number up as long as possible.

Most of these are principles that apply to all kinds of marketing. My problem with many infomercials is that they employ these principles to sell products that have little value.

Infomercials: Where's the Info?

Many infomercial marketers' mission statements must be: "Our mission is to make money by selling product with little or no value." I think we can shoot a little bit higher than this.

The "hit-and-run" feeling I have when watching many infomercials is frightening. I feel an electronic hand reaching into my back pocket. The good news is that the FTC (Federal Trade Commission) is taking a very hard look at the infomercial business. The bad news is that it has had to come to this. The government should not censor infomercials. The producers and television stations should consciously produce responsible programming, without having to be told to by the government.

What's happening is there have been many consumer complaints. Producers have made outrageous claims about their products. The products don't perform. People don't get their money back. The product wasn't shipped in a timely fashion. Poor business practices hurt everyone who is using the medium to market products.

I'm basically a communicator concerned with producing communication pieces that say something and empower people. An infomercial or a television program that doesn't give you something–unless you order the product–really goes against the grain. Why can't an infomercial teach something, give something away, create a bond of trust between the viewer and the presenter? If they buy the product, fine. If not, they still got something of value. Maybe the next time they invite you into their homes they will buy something.

From a marketing point of view, what I do like about infomercials is that you know right away whether or not it works. You test an infomercial in a market or two, and instantly know the results. Either the product was bought, or it wasn't. If the test was successful, the infomercials are rolled out, more time is bought, and more product is sold. The best performing infomercials can sell 10, 20, 30 or 100 million dollars of product in a single year! The flops are instantaneous.

It costs about $25,000 or more to buy enough television time to test an infomercial. With testing, an infomercial can be re-edited and rebroadcast in less than a week to produce more sales. Revamping and publishing a magazine ad takes months. Television is fast. The Home Shopping Network, a kind of continuous infomercial, monitors in real-time the dollars coming in per minute. If sales fall below a certain point–zippo–the old product is history, and a new one is introduced!

When a video is the product, it can be duplicated as the orders come in and shipped very fast to customers. (The packaging must be prepared in advance however.) This means a producer doesn't have to have thousands of dollars tied up in inventory. If the infomercial is a flop, there isn't the problem of liquidating a warehouse full of products.

Who buys from infomercials? Some reports say people between the ages of 25 and 45 with incomes over $20,000. The best selling times are on the weekends and at night when people are less distracted. That's why the airwaves are filled with infomercials on Saturdays and Sundays. The job of the infomercial media buyers is to try to buy the best times to match the demographics of the product to the demographics of the viewing audience.

Not just car wax and cubic zirconias are sold through infomercials. Major national advertisers–car manufacturers and telephone companies–are airing infomercials. In all likelihood, this trend will continue. I only hope that the product really delivers, and that producers start to communicate something through their work. If they are called infomercials, let's see some more information coming through. How about some informational products that improve our educational and health care systems? What about giving somebody something for nothing?

And as I triumphantly step down off of my soapbox, I turn to you and ask "what's your mission statement?" Now go get 'em.

WHAT I'VE LEARNED ABOUT INFOMERCIALS

A Hit!

The first one struck out. The second one is a hit, and already bringing in millions of dollars in its first few months. If I stop producing infomercials now, I'll have the best batting average in the league. (The best infomercial producer around bats .333). But I'm a neophyte infomercial producer, and only make them because they are an effective delivery system for special-interest videos.

When I was VP of original programming at Vestron Video, my job was to identify, develop, produce and manufacture videos that we would sell to wholesalers. They, in turn, would sell to retailers, who then would sell to consumers. It was a tough business, with lots of selling. Think of an hour glass. There are lots of videos at the top and lots of video buyers are the bottom, but getting through that narrow opening in between (selling the wholesalers and retailers) is a large part of the game. It works when you have "A" titles, but even then it's expensive.

Infomercials provide a half-hour opportunity for consumers to "sample" the product. Like CDs played on the radio, audiences can sample the music and then purchase the album if they choose. The longer someone watches an infomercial, the more likely they will be to buy the product.

Infomercials are a kind of "theatrical exposure" for special interest videos. The enormous exposure on television brings tremendous public awareness and creates consumer pull when the video reaches the video stores.

The McDougall Program

The McDougall Program infomercial (on which I was executive producer, writer and director) runs currently on the air on independent stations and cable networks throughout the country. It looks like it may air for a year or more. It sells health information.

Dr. John McDougall runs a health program at St. Helena Hospital in St. Helena, California. He works with people with life-threatening diseases and chronic illnesses, and his treatment includes what is essentially a vegetarian diet. It's not uncommon for his patients to lose weight, lower their blood pressure and cholesterol, and get off medications after two weeks on the diet. Some diseases are actually reversed. This infomercial is kind of a "doc in a box." It's the same 12-day program his patients experience at the clinic, and includes three books (one is a recipe book), an audio tape series, and a video–all for $150.

The opportunity to produce infomercials (and the video, book, and audio products) came at a time when I had just redefined my company's mission statement.

Our mission is to empower and improve
the quality of human life and the environment
by creating worthwhile and educational communication tools.

Infomercials are a perfect marketing vehicle for the health communication tools we produce and publish. An infomercial is part of the distribution and marketing plan. Once an infomercial has run its course, the product is sold in retail outlets with the advantage of having millions of dollars of television exposure.

In my PBS documentaries, I provide hard information. I had hoped to do this with infomercials as well. My rough cut included many of the specific principles of the McDougall Program. Cut out meat, dairy and oil from your diet. Eat fruits and vegetables, and exercise. It appeared too simple. If viewers felt they fully understood what to do, then they didn't need the program. By editing out some of the hard information and by emphasizing expert and real-people testimonials, viewers felt The McDougall Program really offered some life-saving, disease-preventing information.

Claims

When producing infomercials–especially about health–it's critically important to be able to substantiate every claim through sound scientific research documentation. We have two credible medical sources for every claim that we make. If the claim is too speculative, even in a testimonial, we don't use it. Not only are the television stations very leery of programs with outrageous claims, they simply won't air such a show for fear of liability. The FTC (Federal Trade Commission) is especially diligent in making producers back up their claims. The consumer must be protected from fraud.

You can only make claims for results that the average viewer might expect to receive from your product. We have testimonials from people who lost 200 lbs. on The McDougall Program, whose sexual potency returned, or whose breast cancer went into remission. We couldn't, however, use these "miracle stories" because this is not what the average person can expect will happen to them.

What did happen was that people did lose weight, reduced their cholesterol and blood pressure levels, got off medication, and began to feel better–so we emphasized these benefits.

96

Credibility

One element that contributes to the success of the McDougall infomercial is its authenticity. The testimonials are extremely credible. People speak from their experience of using McDougall's information. Almost any skeptic's concerns are defused by the experts' opinions and real-life testimonials. Whether they are young or old, male or female, viewers come to believe that McDougall offers something that works. McDougall himself looks directly into the camera and tells you about his program.

I believe that you have to be authentic. You have to tell the truth. You have to have integrity. People already do not trust television. In fact, statistically, only 15 percent will respond to a television offer. (These numbers are increasing.) The other 85 percent who might be interested want to see it, touch it, and test it in a store before buying it.

Many infomercials are shot before live television audiences to build excitement, or in studio living rooms. Neither approach felt right or "real" for McDougall. To build credibility and believability, I shot the infomercial documentary-style in people's homes, at the clinic, and during Dr. McDougall's radio show.

Strategy

As producers, we come in touch with a lot of information. It is our job to synthesize it, make is visual and auditory, and make it easy to understand. What I now look for are experts/presenters and information that can empower people's lives. Then I see whether it is best presented in a video, a set of audio tapes, books, or all of the above.

Do not think infomercials as a business unto themselves, or you may be very disappointed. The airwaves are very crowded. Top infomercial companies review hundreds of ideas every month. Very few are produced. Media time is getting harder (and more expensive to buy). Major advertisers are entering the field.

Instead, producers should think of infomercials as but one marketing element in a larger strategic plan that takes advantage of the great exposure infomercials can bring to a product.

Until next time, find a worthy project to do as an infomercial–something that really contributes value to people's lives. Now, go get 'em.

You Can Make Desktop Video–But Can You Sell It?

The advice in this column is basically that you need to find the most appropriate distribution channels for your product and make sure that the production value you deliver matches the expectations of your audience.

The title of this column is the crux of the problem. Not a day passes when our consulting office is not asked this question by telephoning producers. And it's always the same problem. They've written, shot or produced material–and they don't know where to sell it. The right time to ask "Where can I sell it?" is when you're first onto a hot new project–not six months later!

I am convinced that you can use desktop video to create broadcast quality television programs. I recently called upon the hardest working man in desktop video," fellow *Videography* columnist Scott Billups. In the course of a few days, we shot, edited, mixed and mastered a half-hour television piece without leaving the room! Furthermore, production speed is hitting an all-time high, while production costs for quality product are plunging.

These savings, however, do not mean that producers no longer have to keep their eye on the marketing outlets for their work. They still have to recoup their blood, sweat and cash somewhere. So, "how do you sell it?"

I turn the discussion back on the producers and ask, "Who is your audience? How can you reach them? What are the distribution channels?" Most of the projects these producers offer are not going to be sold through video stores because they are not movie entertainment. And video stores don't sell much of any other genre than movies. You have to look to other markets to sell most how-to's, documentaries, business or corporate training videos, or the myriad of other hybrid videos which do not yet have a genre.

The business is closer to video publishing than to movie-making. Producers are creating communication pieces–the value of which is usually contained in the information within the video. You can learn how to do something by watching.

So, the questions become "Who is the audience?" "What would they pay for this kind of information?" and "How will they hear about (and subsequently buy) the video product?" You need an answer before you can market your videos.

Video purchasers generally get their information about new video releases through direct-mail pieces, magazine/journal ads, or television spots. For example, the *Lifeguides* documentaries that I produced last year for PBS are marketed through: (1) direct mail pieces to professionals and institutions; (2) reviews, publicity and ads in journals; and (3) a 1-800 number solicitation immediately following the television broadcast. It takes several channels to reach the marketplace.

Your exercise is to find out how your specific audience receives information. Hopefully, your program is priced high, and the marketing costs are low. Sometimes the costs of marketing are too high for low-priced programs, as you can see in the accompanying Direct Marketing Chart.

Pricing is a key issue.

Even with relatively low desktop video budgets you still have advertising, marketing and duplication expenses. (Fortunately, you may not have to duplicate until you have your first batch of orders.) Does your video contain information that is valuable enough for someone to want to pay for it? If so, how high is the perceived value, $19.95?, $99.95? What will people pay? How does the marketplace value other videos?

My advice to consulting clients: If you have a great idea for one tape, what about a series, a product line? Marketing costs are the same for one tape or a dozen tapes. With a line of video product, your average order rises, marketing costs fall, and you have an overall greater profit margin.

(Please note that the chart shows very general numbers. Use the outline if you wish, but you'll have to research your own actual numbers based on your own product and distribution channels. The costs could be higher or lower. The chart's numbers are for demonstration purposes only.)

Let's explore three venues for selling your tape. There's direct mail, where you send out a flyer. There's magazine "per inquiry," where the magazine gives you a free ad in exchange for a share of revenues. And then there's television advertising.

Let's look at two scenarios with a single-tape offering and a three-tape offering. The production budgets will be higher with the three-tape offering, as will duplication and UPS charges–but we'll also be able to increase the retail price on the three-tape offering while everything else stays the same! Your sales strategy might use all three marketing approaches.

Direct Marketing

DIRECT MARKETING						
	Direct Mail		PI:Per Inquiry		TV Spot	
INCOME	*1 Tape*	*3 Tapes*	*1 Tape*	*3 Tapes*	*1 Tape*	*3 Tapes*
Retail Price	$19.95	$99.95	$19.95	$99.95	$19.95	$99.95
Shipping/Handling	3.00	7.00	3.00	7.00	3.00	7.00
Net Per Unit	$22.95	$106.95	$22.95	$106.95	$22.95	$106.95
Duplication	-3.00	-9.00	-3.00	-9.00	-3.00	-9.00
Order Processing	-2.50	-2.50	-2.50	-2.50	-2.50	-2.50
UPS	-2.00	-4.00	-2.00	-4.00	-2.00	-4.00
Credit Card Cost @ 3%	-0.60	-3.00	-0.60	-3.00	-0.60	-3.00
Returns @ 5%	-1.15	-5.35	-1.15	-5.35	-1.15	-5.35
Net Per Unit	$13.70	$83.10	$13.70	$83.10	$13.70	$83.10
MARKETING EXPENSES						
Produce Mailer, Ad or TV Spot	1,000	1,000	1,000	1,000	4,000	4,000
Mailer Cost/30,000	22,500	22,500				
List Purchase @ $0.15	4,500	4,500				
Subscriber/Audience Reach			30,000	30,000	100,000	100,000
TV Spot Buys					1,500	1,500
Total Marketing	$28,000	$28,000	$1,000	$1,000	$5,500	$5,500
REVENUES						
Units Sold to Recover Mkt. Costs	2,043	337	73	12	401	66
Resp Rate to Break Even	6.80%	1.10%	0.20%	0.00%	0.40%	0.10%
Units Sold at 2% Resp.	600	600	600	600		
Units Sold on TV at 1/4% Resp.					250	250
Gross Revenues	$13,770	$64,170	$13,770	$64,170	$5,738	$26,738
Less 15% Magazine Royalty			1,083	7,329		
Net Profit at 2% Response	($19,778)	$21,862	$6,139	$41,533		
At 1/4% Response					($2,074)	$15,276
Marketing as a % of Gross Rev	203%	44%	7%	2%	96%	21%
* Based on 30,000 Magazine Circulation, 2.00% Response Rate, 600 Orders						

You Can Make Desktop Video
But Can You Sell It?

Direct Mail

Let's assume we pay $1000 to have a flyer designed. We print and mail flyers, which cost 75 cents each, to a 30,000-name mailing list which we bought for $4,500. Marketing costs are $28,000. To recover these costs, we have to sell 2,043 single videos or 337 three-video sets.

A good response to a mailing might be two percent. The single-unit video sale requires nearly a seven percent response rate to break even. This is too high to consider. The three-tape offering with a 1.1 percent response rate to break even is a better bet. This analysis tells us you have a better chance of success with a three-tape offering than with the single tape. The marketing costs on the three-tape offering are 44 percent, almost half the retail price. Marketing is expensive.

Per Inquiry

Another scenario that will produce results for little risk is the "P.I.," or per inquiry deal. Since advertising sales are the lowest they've been in a decade, there are publishers willing to cut deals just to get ad pages. Recently we made a P.I. deal with a magazine. We paid for the full-page ad design and mechanicals. In exchange, the magazine receives 15 percent of gross sales (not including shipping or taxes). They ran the ad for three months, and it was so successful they've just extended it for another six months. For us, there was little risk, and the ad produced supplemental sales revenues with no more investment than the cost of the mechanical.

In our video example, we pay $1000 for the ad's design and mechanicals. We make money (less 15 percent) very quickly with 0.02 percent response rate. If we get a 2 percent response rate, some income will go to the magazine publisher, and they may continue running the ad. Now is a particularly good time to try this strategy with magazines.

Television Spots

Television is much more risky, because you have to find a television audience that will respond to your tape offering. A highly rated show–even in a local market–might be prohibitively expensive. Let's assume we produce a TV spot for $4000, and we buy $1500 worth of ads to test our offering. Only on the three-tape offering do we make money, and this is with a 0.25 percent response rate. If the test is successful, more television time will be bought.

There's hardly enough space here to go into all the different strategies that could be employed for selling desktop video productions, but this will give you some idea of the possibilities. I invite you to combine these and other marketing avenues, especially publicity (which is sometimes free), in selling your desktop videos. Now go get 'em.

GETTING A BIG BANG FOR THE BUCK:
"THE ASTRONOMERS"

This is one of my favorite marketing examples. It demonstrates that you can take a very difficult subject (science videos!) and through the integration and synergy of various elements, inspire everyone's participation in a very esoteric product, and sell a lot of units.

It was a first! The home video and book release would occur simultaneously with the April 25th PBS broadcast of the limited series *The Astronomers*. The manufacturers of three different products–a television series, a video collection, and a book–would create national awareness for their individual products by working together.

As a consultant to PBS Home Video (which is distributed exclusively by Pacific Arts Video ([213] 657-2233), I was assigned to coordinate the marketing plan for the video release of *The Astronomers*.

A Perfect Universe

This wasn't the first time I've worked on cross-promotions with publishers, record companies and broadcasters. At the outset, everyone usually says, "Yeah, great, we'll work together." But by the time the release rolls around, everyone is off on their own agenda, and the potential marketing synergy dissipates. *The Astronomers* was an exception. Everyone worked extremely well together. In fact, television and video producers of new works can look to *The Astronomers* as a kind of perfect case study of what can happen when marketers work together.

So far, the sales response from the field has been tremendous, and it looks like sales goals will be met or surpassed. What follows are some of the marketing elements and ideas which came together to create what at this moment looks to be a phenomenal success story.

The Astronomers is a six-hour limited series which profiles the lives and work of scientists revolutionizing our knowledge of the universe. The series is narrated by Richard Chamberlain and was produced on a $5 million grant from the W. M. Keck Foundation by Los Angeles PBS station KCET. It aired April 15th over PBS national and will continue for five subsequent Mondays.

Synergetic Relationships

Public Television is airing the series. PBS Home Video will sell the six-volume video "collector's edition" to video stores. PBS Video (the non-theatrical distributor) is selling the video to the educational and institutional markets. And St. Martin's Press is publishing the companion book. In our initial meetings, we emphasized a desire to promote *The Astronomers* as a "multi-media" event. In this way, each marketer could reap the benefits of everyone's efforts and could maximize their own sales through the tremendous, accumulative publicity and promotion.

If we worked together, we could economize, best employ our resources, and hopefully, avoid duplicating efforts. We could go to the press in a coordinated manner. (Three sets of publicists representing KCET, PBS Home Video, and the St. Martin's Press worked together so that three publicists weren't going to the same editors.) This meant that a publicity "hit list" could be divided, increasing efficiency and results.

Key Art

One of the most important coordinated pieces was <u>the design of a single piece of key art,</u> which was used for all media. (The book and the video used the key art on the covers. The broadcaster used the key art in newspaper ads.) To use different art would diminish consumer awareness and would be detrimental to all. The multiple impressions on viewers and consumers results in greater awareness. By the third time they've seen the art, they may respond by buying a book, purchasing a video, or tuning into the program. The key art was a man and a woman (astronomers presumably) next to the Palomar Observatory dome looking at the moon. The beauty of this art is that it works well in both a poster or postage-stamp size, which can be used in both horizontal and vertical formats.

The Video

Each individual title sells for $19.95 retail. The six-volume set sells for $129.95. If you bought them separately it would cost $119.70. What would, in the words of a marketer, "add value" to the set, so that a consumer would spend $10.25 more for the collection? Answering this question was one of my tasks. Taking a lesson from *The Civil War* set, we licensed, re-published, and reduced a 48-page book, *Your Personal Guide to the Night Sky*, to fit inside the attractive video gift pack. Added value!

One primary promotable element in *The Astronomers* is the $1 million special effects. To get a bigger bang for the buck, we edited these effects together in a seven-minute "music video" –the ultimate space trip. Inside the "collector's edition" set, consumers will find a coupon to send away to get their free "music video." More value!

In addition, you receive other coupons which grant you a discount on 1) membership in the Astronomical Society of the Pacific, 2) a subscription to *Omni Magazine*, and 3) a discount on their own telescope. Even more value. Wow!

Selling the Sellers

A major ad and promotion campaign in *The New Yorker, People, Omni, Premiere, Scientific American, Life* and other national magazines should send customers flocking to video stores, bookstores and mass merchant outlets. But how do you get the video stores to carry the product?

You have to sell the sellers. With hundreds of new video products each month to choose from, and limited dollars, the video retailers must choose *The Astronomers* video product over someone else's. The goal of PBS Home Video is to sell units. In order to incentivize video stores to buy more titles, a large floor display with 24 titles was created. When the retailer bought the floor display, they got a free all-purpose telescope.

This did the trick! Store buyers wanted the free telescope to keep themselves, to give away to their sales people, or to offer to their customers through a drawing. Some saw how they could also use this free gift as a temporary floor display to help draw attention to *The Astronomers* videos. (To get the lowest possible price on telescopes, we bought in volume and told them a discount coupon would be inserted in every tape set. They went for it. After all, the tapes will reach an audience most interested in telescopes. In return, they agreed to stuff their telescope boxes with *The Astronomers* sales sheets. A perfect, target audience for videos. Everyone wins.

Cross Marketing and Coordination

There are numerous markets for a tape collection like *The Astronomers*. The most targeted are those with a strong interest in astronomy. These are the folks that would plunk down $129.95 for the entire series. But how do you get to them? In order for people to respond even to something they may be interested in, you have to get to them frequently and in many ways.

In order to take advantage of the six-week period when the programs would be on PBS, I wrote a "Special Astronomers Edition" of the PBS Home Video Newsletter. This newsletter is designed to create a dialogue between video stores and PBS Home Video. The notion is that if you give retailers good marketing tips and ideas on how they can more successfully sell the PBS line of home videos, you build loyalty. They will buy more PBS Home Video titles. The Special Issue was sent to 70,000 video outlets, and 350 observatories/planetariums, and 300 PBS stations. The newsletter featured marketing tips on <u>how video outlets, planetariums, and PBS stations could work together</u>.

Although each is driven by self-interest and has a slightly different agenda, everyone can win. PBS can attract more people who may potentially become station members (e.g. contribute money). PBS Home Video can sell more videos. And the observatories can take advantage of all the publicity surrounding *The Astronomers* by creating workshops, seminars and other events as the public gets excited about astronomy.

Planetariums may get more attendees and members. For example, the newsletter suggests that local video stores call up their amateur astronomy clubs and invite them to bring their telescopes to the video store parking lot for a "Star Gazing Party." Such an event would certainly merit publicity in the local media and would help draw people into the video store.

A major event like this requires an extraordinary amount of planning; it doesn't just happen. Hopefully, some of these ideas will fuel your own imaginations when it comes to marketing and cross-marketing your programs. Now go get 'em.

DISTRIBUTION

SELF-DISTRIBUTION

The Kantola Brothers are hot. They're focused, and they're profitable. Model yourself after those who have mastered the playing field, and add years to your life!

The Kantola Brothers: self distribution has led their company to $3 million in sales.

With the plethora of low-cost production technologies available, there are a lot of producers out there who feel they could market and distribute their own programs. Everyone has thought of doing this at one time or another. You may have created something that no distributor will take, or feel that you could do a better job marketing your video title. Maybe you want to make more than the traditional video royalty.

For some, it's the right move. For others, the constant attention to customer service, marketing, promotion, duplication and shipping may be enough to drive them right back onto location. What follows is the story of one company, Kantola Productions, for whom self distribution was definitely the right move.

Steve and Rick Kantola formed the video production and marketing company that bears their name several years ago. As a two (now seven) person operation, they took destiny into their own hands and produced one, and then a line of, video programs–creating a quiet but successful distribution company. This year Kantola Productions, based in San Francisco, will have sales reaching approximately $3 million. How did they do it?

Using their story as a case study, I'll identify some principles that may help you in your own distribution efforts.

1.   Start Small, Have A Strategy, and Bootstrap Your Way To Success.

The Kantolas produced a video titled *Toastmasters Be Prepared to Speak* in 1985. Rick was the Researcher/Writer and worked with an organization known as Toastmasters to develop the script. Steve served as Producer and is now Marketer/Distributor of this and an entire line of Toastmaster video programs. Toastmaster was not paid any fees during development or production. They do, however, now receive a royalty on tape sales. The Kantola's self-financed the $50,000 budget and worked with an experienced production team to produce the first half-hour program.

2.   Make the Owner of the Content and Core Audience Your Partner.

The "how to" nature of learning how to speak in public is ideal for video because you can see how–and how not–to give a speech. It's informative, entertaining and dramatic.

3.   Be Sure The Content Works Well in Video.

Viewers go through every step of learning how to give a speech, from speech writing, to practicing, and delivering their words. The video is a comprehensive approach to the art of how to give a speech–a skill needed by almost every business person today.

4.   The More Needed the Skill or Information, the Greater the Market.

The initial program was sold at $79.95 and sells today for $89.95 with a 32-page study guide. When the tape was first produced, there were only a few similar tapes on the market, and those had higher price points.

5.   Research Similar Titles–Look Before You Leap.

Today there are several $29.95 "speech" tapes in the marketplace, but the producers have inappropriately selected consumer distribution. This is a very tough way to go because: (1) there are many movie titles competing for shelf space, and (2) the producers must sell at a low price point when actually the market will bear a higher price. The consumer-oriented "speech" titles have had little success.

6.   When You Get A Hit, Create Sequels.

Once it was clear that *Be Prepared to Speak* had found an audience, the Kantolas developed three new titles that could be marketed to the same buyers. These included *Be Prepared to Lead*, *Be Prepared To Sell*, and *Be Prepared for Meetings*.

7.   Pick the Right Channels of Distribution.

Through Steve Kantola's efforts, 60,000 units of their program have been sold. And, as they get better at opening up channels of distribution, sales increase each year.

8.   Keep Working Your Title.

Steve emphasized that they are "very careful" and "give full attention to all the details." He says, "when we started we were undercapitalized and had to be very careful. If we had started with all the money we needed, we probably would have made expensive mistakes early and been out of business today."

9.   Start Small Until You Learn the Business.

The good news for producers, then, is that in most cases they have to start small. Lean and mean is a great teacher, because you must be innovative and employ low-cost guerrilla marketing techniques. You can't buy an ad in *People* magazine, so you have to get customers in clever and effective ways. The Kantolas started small, "in a low-profile office and without much of a phone system" and have built a very successful small business.

10.   Self-Distribution Means Do It Yourself.

The two-person operation must go through all the steps from brochure design, copy writing, getting it printed, buying lists, and doing the mailings. (The Kantolas also hire graphic artists to tweak their designs and employ a mailing house in Oregon to do the mailings.)

11.   Hire Professional Help When Needed.

They also do their own order fulfillment. When testing a mailer or sales offering, they may select as few as 2500 names from four or five lists. Strangely enough, Steve says, "Tests do better than roll-outs and no one knows exactly why." So even though you may identify a strong list, you may not get the exact percentage return as the test. Once the test is successful, then all the names from the list will be used. Lists that do not perform well will not be used any further.

12.   Tests–Walk Before You Run.

Mailing pieces, in quantities of 10,000, may cost $1 each, or a total of $10,000. A one percent return would be 100 sales. For an $89 tape, the mailing would gross $89,000. A half-percent return would gross less than $45,000. Subtract other costs, such as duplicating, shipping and handling, overhead and program production, and you quickly see how little is left as "net profit." This emphasizes the importance of testing. The difference between the right list and the wrong list is the difference between success and failure.

As the business grows and you gain confidence in mailing hundreds of thousands of flyers at a time, the price for an eight-page color mailer can fall to 30 to 60 cents. Thus your cost per order will fall accordingly. A strong list and high volume mailer can increase your profit margin.

13.   Identify as Many Distribution Channels as Possible.

Besides selling directly through the mail to individuals and corporate buyers, the Kantolas also sell through distributors–mostly catalogers–who feature videos in their own direct-mail catalogs. The catalogs buy the videos at a 40 percent discount.

Self-distribution works best once you discover several different channels of distribution. You then begin to market to each, gaining larger and larger entry into those channels. Kantola Productions videos are sold through these channels: 20 percent through display ads; 10 percent through catalogs/distributors; and 10 percent through joint venture and newsletter.

14.   Know Your Buyer, and Market to That Buyer.

It is important to identify your buyer and find ways to communicate directly and effectively to that buyer. The more you sell, the more you will come to know who the buyers are. And in doing that, you can refine the copy and design of your mail piece and improve your ability to communicate the benefits of your program. Kantola has found that his video buyers are both middle and upper-level executives ("given the benefits, it's not an expensive product"), university professors, high school professors or "anyone who teaches public speaking."

15.   Produce Programs That Have A Long Shelf Life.

It's cheaper to work out your ideas on paper before you start shooting. It's easy to be seduced by ideas during a cappuccino rush. Wait. Think about the criteria of your product. Is it a short, fad-type subject that–in two years –will be of interest to no one? Or is it "evergreen," and will be used for a long time? If your subject is of general interest, all the better. If it has a pre-promoted name, subject or celebrity attached, all the better again. There is nothing wrong with producing a tape on a "hot" subject, but you must have a marketing and distributing channel that can get the "hot" tape out before it turns "cold." You could be left with a warehouse full of Milli Vanilli.

In the Kantolas' case, they selected an "evergreen" subject that will be of interest all year long, for many years. Basically, the content (public speaking) is timeless. The only thing that may need to be updated from decade to decade is the clothes his subjects wear.

The secret to the whole operation, according to the Kantolas, is to stick to the basics. For them that is: (1) a name product (Toastmasters), (2) a title with great general interest, and (3) a low price point (in comparison to what a professional seminar consultant would cost).

114

Self Distribution

16.   Select A Marketing Partner.

Select a strategic marketing partner that can help you start off strongly. This partner may have access to content or proprietary information (for development into video) and to a mailing list, magazine or newsletter to get to a large target market. "Toastmasters," says Steve, "is a great organization. They helped develop the program. They wanted the exposure, and it was a good thing for their 170,000 members. They helped us bring the video to the market in the beginning."

17.   Build A Database of Your Buyers.

Building from a core audience, Kantola began developing a mailing list of individuals, educators and businesses interested in his videos. As he developed new and similar titles, he could go back to his previous customers. He is always expanding his database. Now he sends out 1.5 million mailings per year. A one percent return would yield 15,000 orders.

18.   Develop Customer Loyalty.

Kantola has focused on the kind of information his customers want. Experience has taught him who his buyers are so that he can send his mailer to the right person in the corporation.

19.   Master One Line Before Going on to Others.

From the experience of developing one successful line, Kantola has also produced four business training videos in cooperation with the Wharton School of the University of Pennsylvania. The Kantolas are applying what they've learned to new lines of video product. Kantola Productions is probably just one of many quiet success stories. If you have a story to tell, please send me a letter.

Now, for the rest of you who may just be dreaming about "doing it yourself," I hope that you may absorb and test some of these principles and use them to successfully develop your own channels of distribution. Now go get 'em.

THE HIT LIST

Got a program that deserves widespread distribution, but don't know where to go to make that happen? This column frequently deals with techniques for marketing your video. This time it features a list of companies that video producers might want to use to begin their search for a distributor for direct-to-home video programs as well as business, corporate or educational videos.

There are hundreds of distributors. The list that follows is only a place to begin–not a recommendation of any particular distributor. It's up to you to find the best match between your program and the abilities of the distributor. Take your time and be careful in your selection. A distribution deal is usually a long-term marriage, five to seven years. So do your homework, and get it right. Each distributor has a personality, a different market share, and a different marketing approach. Many distributors enter and leave the market quickly. By the time you use this list, many may have moved, gone out of business, or changed phone numbers. This list is comprised of two kinds of distributors: home video and institutional/educational.

"Home video" suppliers are those companies that acquire, and sometimes finance, videos intended for the direct-to-the-home market. The suppliers manufacture the tapes, develop marketing materials, and sell their tapes to retail outlets (which rent and/or sell tapes) to consumers. Most sell the videos through wholesalers and sell direct to the larger retail accounts. The core of the direct-to-the-home business continues to be movies. But many of these suppliers also distribute "special interest programs," which can include genres such as how-to, children's, exercise, music and other non-movie programs. Generally the retail selling price is in the $9.95 to $29.95 range to consumers. Depending on the price point, producers can expect a 10-20 percent royalty based on gross receipts. For a further explanation of how this all works, I recommend you read my book, *Film and Video Marketing*.

"Industrial, corporate, or educational" video refers to those distributors that acquire and sometimes finance videos for sale to institutions. Many corporate training videos are distributed by these companies. Price points range from $99 to $9,999. Sales of a few hundred to a few thousand tapes is considered good, depending on the production budget and marketing costs. The list contains some of names of people who can help you.

How to Use the "Hit List."

1. Ascertain whether your program or proposed program is best suited for home video distribution or business/corporate use.
2. See the appropriate list.

117

3. Begin calling the distributors. Ask for their catalogs. Ask if their company handles your type of program (e.g., a computer training tape, a time management tape, etc.). If not, ask for the names of other distributors who do handle that kind of program.

4. Review the catalogs of the companies who handle programs similar to yours. Assess whether you like their pricing, marketing style and the other aspects you see.

5. Call the company's acquisitions or program development or marketing director. Explain what you've got. Make your pitch concise, to the point, and in the language and style of the catalog. By making sure you are pitching to a qualified buyer, you have a much better chance of finding distribution for your program. If they are interested, they will request that you send your proposal or finished tape for their review.

6. All companies are different. Some will "review" your program for months, others–if they perceive it to be a highly marketable idea or tape–will get back to you immediately.

7. If you've gotten this far, you very possibly will start negotiating to obtain the best possible deal you can. It may involve a cash advance against royalties, an ongoing royalty, a marketing commitment, or any number of other features.

You will probably get lot of "no's" along the way. Don't fret, because every "no" you get just might bring you closer to an eventual "yes." Now go get 'em!

Home Video Suppliers

Best Film and Video Corp., 20501 Ventura Blvd., #195, Woodland Hills, CA 91364, (818) 999-2244. Also 108 New South Road, Hicksville, NY, 11801 (800) 527-2189

BMG Distribution, 6363 Sunset Blvd., Hollywood, CA 90028, (213) 468-4069

Cabin Fever Entertainment, One Sound Shore Drive, Cos Cob, CT 06830, (203) 622-0595

CBS/Fox Video, Acquisitions Dept, 1330 Avenue of the Americas, New York, NY 100319, (212) 373-4800

Coliseum Video, 430 West 54th St., New York, NY 10019, (212) 489-8156
Direct Cinema Limited, P.O. Box 10003, Santa Monica CA 90410, (310) 396-4774

Columbia/Tri-Star Home Video, 3400 Riverside Drive, Burbank, CA 91505, (818) 972-8686

Disney Home Video, 500 South Buena Vista St., Burbank, CA 91521, (818) 562-3650

Do-It-Yourself, PO Box 910, Oriental, NC 28203, (704) 342-9608

HBO Video Inc., 1100 6th Avenue, New York NY 10036, (212) 512-7400

Image Entertainment (laserdiscs), 9333 Oso Ave, Chatsworth, CA 91311, (818) 407-9100

J2 Communications, 10850 Wilshire Blvd., Suite 1000, Los Angeles, CA 90024, (310) 474-5252

Kultur, 121 Highway 36, West Long Branch, NJ 07764, (908) 229-2337

Live Home Video & Family Home Entertainment, 15400 Sherman Way, PO Box 10124, Van Nuys, CA 91410, (818) 988-5060

MCA /Universal Home Video, 100 Universal City Plaza, Universal City, CA 91608, (818) 777-1000

MGM Home Video, 10000 West Washington Blvd., Culver City, CA 90232, (310) 280-6000

Mystic Fire Video, 225 Lafayette St., #1206, New York, NY 10012, (212) 941-0999

NFL Films, 330 Fellowship Road, Mount Laurel, NJ 08054, (609) 778-1600

Pacific Arts Video, 11858 La Grange Ave., Los Angeles CA 90025, (310) 820-0991

Paramount Home Video, 5555 Melrose Ave., Los Angeles, CA 90038, (213) 956-5000

PBS Home Video, 11858 La Grange Ave., Los Angeles, CA 90025, (310) 820-0991

Pioneer Laserdisc Corp. of America, 2265 E. 220 St., Long Beach, CA 90810, (310) 835-6177

Prism Entertainment, 1888 Century Park East, Suite 350, Los Angeles, CA 90067, (310) 277-3270

Republic Pictures, 12636 Beatrice St., Los Angeles, CA 90066, (310) 306-4040

Rhino Video, 10635 Santa Monica Blvd, CA 90025 (310)474-4778

Sony Video, P.O. Box 4450, Room 51-4, New York, NY 10101, (212) 445-5295

Turner Entertainment Company, 420 Fifth Ave., New York, NY 10018, (212) 852-6600

The Voyager Company (laserdiscs, CD-ROMS), 1351 Pacific Coast Highway, Santa Monica, CA 90401, (310) 451-1383

Warner Home Video, 4000 Warner Blvd., Burbank, CA 91522-0001, (818) 954-6000

Wood Knapp & Company, 5900 Wilshire Blvd., Los Angeles CA 90036, (213)549-3500

Non-Theatrical Suppliers

Aims Media, 9710 DeSoto Ave., Chatsworth, CA 91311, (818) 773-4300

American Media Inc., 4900 University Ave., West Des Moines, IA 50266, (800) 262-2557

Barr Films and Barr Entertainment, 12801 E. Schabarum Ave., Irwindale, CA 91706, (818) 338-7878

BFA Educational Media, 2349 Chassee Drive, St. Louis, MO 63146, (314) 569-0211

Cambridge Career Products, P.O. Box 2153, Charleston, WV 25328, (800) 468-4227

Coronet/MTI, 108 Wilmot Road, Deerfield, IL 60015, (800) 621-2131

Dartnell Corp., 4660 N. Ravenswood, Chicago, IL 60640, (800) 621-5463

Films for the Humanities and Sciences, P.O. Box 2053, Princeton, NJ 08543, (609) 452-1128

Films Inc./PMI, 5547 North Ravenswood Ave., Chicago, IL 60640, (800) 323-4222

Medical Electronic Education Service, 1560 Sherman Ave., Evanston, IL 60201, (800) 323-9084

Modern Talking Picture Service, 5000 Park St. North, St. Petersburg, FL 33709, (800) 237-7114

Nightingale-Conant Corp., 7300 N. Lehigh Ave., Niles, IL 60714, (800) 572-2770

PBS Video, 1320 Braddock Pl., Alexandria, VA 22314, (800) 424-7963

Perennial Education Inc., 1560 Sherman Avenue, Suite 100, Evanston, IL 60201, (708) 328-6700

Pyramid Film And Video, P.O. Box 1048, Santa Monica, CA 90406, (310) 828-7577

Spinnaker Software, 201 Broadway, Cambridge, MA 02139, (617) 494-1200

University of California Extension, Center for Media and Independent Learning, 2176 Shattuck Ave., Berkeley, CA 94704, (510) 642-0460

NEW MEDIA

NEW MEDIA: NEW SPOUSE?

I am already spending too much time in front of monitors. And I don't mean television. With a new baby in the house it is clear to me that there are other priorities. Besides shouldn't we ask ourselves some big questions about all this technology before we so quickly embrace it?

They wanted me to speak. In two days I was to be on panel entitled "Studios, Independents, Networks and New Media" at a conference held locally. I didn't know what to say.

The moderator asked me to consider what the future relationships between independent producers and the studios will be with the new media. He asked, "With the new media, will there be a different relationship than currently exists between producers and studios, between recording artists and labels, between authors and publishers?" My answer: "I don't think so." It's going to be a very short panel.

Let's look to history to understand my answer. When cable television, and later home video, began to develop, the studios didn't pay much attention until they began to see an erosion of their audiences. Then they moved in. It was time for vertical integration. Today, the lion's share of home video revenues go to the majors. Yes, there are some independents who have been able to hang on, but the majors are the ones who control distribution.

With the new media there will initially be a plethora of players trying to create new standards, proprietary hardware, and software, but this will ultimately shake down to large conglomerates that will acquire the smaller companies whose services and products prove worthy. There may be some surprises as the phone companies enter the playing field, but ultimately the winners will be absorbed by the multinationals.

Why should we expect that new media should bring about any profound changes in the way Hollywood does business? The president of the conference I planned to speak at talked about the day when "a JFK interactive might be able to bring in $40 million to a studio." Industry speculators expect interactive media to build new divisions within the film and music industries. I'm sure that will happen. The media formats may change, but will the relationship between the video producer and the financier/distributor change? There is no reason to assume it will.

I think somewhere along the line, however, we missed asking the first question—way before what profits we will see, way before how much money the studios will make, and way before who the new players will be. We missed the most basic question: "Is new media such a great thing and why? Or why not?" Is anyone asking this question?

What's So Great About the New Media?

It's fun. You can do more. We all know what's great about the new media because every ad or review or brochure we read tells us the upside. Each month this magazine reports on desktop video, but that's just part of the larger "multimedia" scene. Each month I rush to open *Videography* and my stack of computer magazines to see the latest and the greatest.

But in this rush I fear we do not ask ourselves some important questions. After all, we are in the courtship phase of a new relationship with technology, which results in us bringing the new media into our homes and our lives. From all accounts, we are going to be spending a lot of time with it. You could even think of the new media as a "new spouse." (Now there's a concept!) For our kids, a multimedia PC with reference works, interactive instruction, and games can become an "imaginary friend." Shouldn't we be concerned about choosing a spouse for ourselves and a friend for our children? Of course. But where is the new media watchdog? Can we at least see a medical and psychological history of the new spouse?

Consider: Video data terminals emit a range of electromagnetic radiation. Long-term users can experience health problems. People on average already watch television nearly eight hours a day, more time than they spend on any other activity. People relate to the events and people of television as if they were real. Reality and fantasy are blending. We have lost touch with one another. The high-speed ability of the new media, information gathering, processing and communication has sped up the world. There is tremendous stress in our lives as a result of new media's pace. We have lost touch with natural rhythms.

Yes, the new media offers great financial opportunities. Yes, you may have more new toys on your desktop than you ever imagined. And yes, like the automobile, there may be psychological, communal and environmental fallout that we should think about now before rushing head-over-heels toward the new technology. Technology isn't good just because it is new. Yet somehow we forget this and find ourselves on a kind of Divine Mission. Let's really look at who benefits (and who doesn't) from the proliferation of new media.

Don't get me wrong. I don't plan to stop producing television, videos or other media. But I do plan to examine the long-term effects of what I am doing. I do care about the end result. I want to leave something behind of value. I have personally seen enormous changes throughout the world as a result of our technology. Thinking about the effects of our actions seven generations ahead has great merit. It's worth applying. With technology exploding, with multinationals getting larger and larger, where do we fit in?

124

What Does the Video Producer Bring to the Party?

The second question we can be asking ourselves is "What can the creative individual bring to the new media party that the large corporations and studios cannot?" And the answer is an old one, which bears repeating: Ideas. The corporations will always need ideas. And because business people are trapped in a corporate-culture fish tank, there will always be individuals outside the corporation that can outthink and out-create them. But ideas themselves are not enough, because ideas are not copyrightable.

You need to put your idea into a form (whether it's a video, a CD-I, a software program, or a movie) that can be copyrighted. Then it is yours, and you have the property which (presumably) cannot be stolen. You are then in the catbird seat, and can go to the studio or multimedia conglomerate with something that you own. If they want it, they have to deal with you. This is one of the ways that an independent producer can establish a meaningful relationship with a larger entity. The independent producer is dependent on the studio for financing and distribution, and the studio is dependent on the producer for the property rights.

Add to your property a new way of telling a story or sharing information (through a multimedia format), and the independent producer can leverage an even greater position. You may have created an authoring system or a special effect. You may bring particular graphic style or sensibility to the property. All these elements will enhance the value of your position with the studios and corporations. Keep asking yourself, "What can I provide that the studios cannot?" You'll find plenty. It's easy to get intimidated when you walk through Paramount's gates until you look down at the property under your arm that bears your copyright. Remember you can always "just say no."

Hey, maybe I had something to say to this panel after all. And I did. In the meantime, go get 'em.

AFI/APPLE LAB: VIDEO BAUHAUS

This is one of the first articles written in 1991 about the AFI Computer Center, now a hot digital video showcase in Los Angeles. You can take classes there with masters of production. You can also attend media salons, and see the latest demos. The vision for the center as discussed in this article was surpassed shortly after its first anniversary!

If you live in or visit L.A., you can't afford not to stop at the AFI. (Read the Digital Jam Session article to get a feel for what goes on there.)

The two voices in my head chatter something like this:

"Hey, I could use my Mac for editing and for creating an animated title sequence. I'd save bucks, and I could do it all at home!"

"Yeah, but if you foul it up and it doesn't work, you'll just have to do it over again."

"But it might look cooler than the Harry and certainly cheaper, and no one would have seen this look before.."

"Go ahead if you want, but you're on a real tight deadline. This is a real important job, and if you screw it up....."

And so what happens is that fear rises and keeps us from trying new things. But production is exactly the time to quit dreaming about new technology and <u>really use it</u>. You've got a production budget!

But where do you go to learn? Who else has worked with computers and video? How can you improve your learning curve? The answer is to go to the AFI/Apple Center in Los Angeles.

Jean Firstenberg and James Hindman of the American Film Institute (AFI) and John Sculley, chairman/CEO of Apple Computer Inc., are creating the AFI/Apple Center though a collaborative effort. Apple donated the computer hardware and the AFI contributed space, staff and expertise. (The Sony Institute of Applied Video Technology is also housed at the AFI.)

I recently met with 50 film and video professionals at the AFI, and we collectively shared a vision for the Center. We all have varying degrees of experience with computers and a passion to learn more. Members of the AFI/Apple Center Steering Committee include fellow columnist Scott Billups, motion-picture consultant Michael Backes, Robert Greenberg of R/Greenberg Associates, Post Group VP Linda Carol Rheinstein, storyboard consultant Van Ling, and software developer David Sosnawe. Our job is to dream a little to come up with what this facility can be, and then put it together. We'll need to raise funds, solicit hardware and software, and gain other support from the professional community. The AFI and Apple have gotten things off to a good start. Now it's up to the rest of us (and perhaps you too) to figure out what to do with this opportunity.

I, like many of the others on the committee, see this as a kind of "Bauhaus of the Nineties." But instead of fine and applied arts converging, now it's computer and film/video technologies. It is apparent that these two worlds depend heavily on one another.

As video futurist, Eric Martin said earlier in the year:

"We're really on the lip of an abyss. We're in for some profound changes. The computer is replacing all tools because it increasingly <u>is</u> all tools. In the digital universe, a sound-is-a-tool-is-an-image-is-a-word-is-a-movement. Since it is all one language, the boundaries between media begin to blur. We're becoming one technology, one medium, and indeed, one decentralizing, interconnecting world culture, and a lot of that is because of this technology."

Just as the technology is converging, so are the interests of a wide range of film, television and video industry heavyweights who make up the AFI/Apple Center advisory committee. They include Michael Crichton, George Spiro Dibie, John Dykstra, Richard Edland, Herbie Hancock, Bob Stein, Michael Nesmith and 40 others.

On the day of our meeting, the large group broke down into smaller groups and brainstormed ideas for the Center.

Feature film director John Badham said: "We're very much in a time of transition, like going from horse-and-buggy to automobile. One key role for the Center is to help guide the transition into computerization for the film and television community. There are those who are actively participating in the change. There are others who know it's happening and want a better understanding. There are others, most people in fact, who don't even know that blacksmiths are on the way out."

Central notions that came out of these sessions were that the AFI/Apple Center can hold public seminars, symposia, conferences and other educational activities that can help expose the new technology and its applications to the creative film/video community. The groups also emphasized that training activities were necessary for both entry-level practitioners and the more intense high-end users. Working professionals can also meet to share ideas and explore state-of-the-art solutions. New groups will be formed to help define the new activities in future meetings.

There were also a number of companies and organizations that wanted to co-sponsor educational activities with the Center, either for their own members and employees to improve their skills, or as a way to increase the overall trained pool of professionals familiar with emerging technologies. A primary need that was identified was that there are simply not enough trained individuals who know how to use the emerging technologies in film and video production.

In a poll of the advisory committee, it was learned that computers are already being used for financial budgeting and reporting, project organization, presentations, music composition, publishing, storyboarding, pre-producing, production, post production, training, multimedia production, sound production, membership database, motion control of cameras, book publishing, electronic intermediate manipulation of image, scriptwriting, image creation, and integrated computer networks tied to design, animation, motion control, (CAD-CAM), modelmaking, editorial, image processing, illustration, live-action, video and options.

One major goal of the Center will be to create liaisons between developers (of hardware and software) and (film/video) producers. An immediate goal is to get the hardware and software companies to move toward integration. The group agreed that there are many terrific programs and systems, but they cannot be linked or fully integrated at present.

It is a most exciting time to be involved with all these imaginative thinkers and doers. Everyone was stimulated, and many ideas were floated. People who knew one another only by reputation were able to meet, and, in some cases, new collaborations were formed. It felt like the Sixties; you had the feeling anything was possible.

The dream is to create "the production facility of the future." (Download, produce and upload your next feature!) With the high intentioned brain power assembled, and the support from the AFI and Apple, there's no reason why this can't happen. Film and videomakers are among the first to recognize that if you can dream it, then you can do it. Now go get 'em.

(AFI/Apple Center director is Nick DeMartino at (213) 856-7690.)

THE MAC AND I: SOMETHING FROM NOTHING

My Mac and I wait for the Muse. As she arrives, electro-chemical impulses bolt through my brain, speed through the ends of my fingers, and rest as charged bits on Mac's hard disk. To inspire and move our audience, we gather, access and process volumes of information.

Long ago I gave up the limiting title of videomaker for the much more expansive moniker of communicator. And wonderful things happened. I began to express myself in a variety of forms–not just video!

And as a communicator, I owe a lot to the Mac and how it has empowered me to organize and process information. And that's what this column is about–the communication process. A metaphysical happening, because when you really think about it, we are really making something out of nothing.

Stage One

We choose to create something. If we have a "vision," then having already seen the outcomes we can proceed in a very focused manner. Perhaps it's just a notion. We conceive.

Stage Two

We gather information, images and sound. The Mac is the warehouse for all notes, ideas, text and images. All relevant names and phone numbers are logged onto a database.

Stage Three

We access this information. We know who to talk to and where to go to get information. I may use the Mac's modem to research online data bases, to send and receive graphics, scripts and treatments. The modem, phone and fax have replaced many in-person meetings. Many people who work with me do so from their Macs in their own homes. We meet in a "virtual office" on the computer screen!

Stage Four

At some point we have to stop accessing and begin to process the voluminous text, images and sounds we've collected. Depending on the medium, this stage may include writing, rewriting, polishing, recording, editing, mixing, animating, mastering and duplicating.

Stage Five

We communicate through the fruit of our labor–a communication piece–usually a product through which we can share our knowledge. It could be a video, a book or a CD. Or a phone call, a modem transmission, a seminar. To communicate, we may also market, promote and distribute the product.

Throughout the entire process, there are also a myriad of other Mac-produced "communication pieces" such as photographs, pitches, presentations, proposals, drawings, illustrations, budgets, deal memos, contracts, scripts, resource guides, typography, titles, sales sheets, covers, advertisements, packaging, press releases, reports, memos, letters, faxes and phone calls.

It's incredible. The central tool for organizing, processing and sharing information is the computer. Yet I don't consider myself in the computer business. In 1976 P.M. (pre Mac), this process was far more cumbersome. I needed lots of time and assistants to gather and process information. Today–thanks to my Mac IIci with its peripherals and programs–I can do more with less. And it's fun. When I turn on my computer, the first file that is displayed is labeled play. I am programming my unconscious and conscious mind to enjoy whatever I am doing.

I am always learning new uses for the Mac. It's tremendously exciting. If you haven't already taken the plunge, do so. Start using computers. Learn as much as you can. If you already use them, expand your abilities. Find out how other communicators are using computers to create. Take classes at such places as the Los Angeles-based American Film Institute's Apple Media Lab or sit at the feet of other Mac buffs. You'll find your power to communicate will expand exponentially. Now go get 'em.

CD-I 4 ME?

New formats like CD-I made me feel insecure. Should I think about producing CD-I's? To answer that question, I reviewed many CD-I's and wrote this article. However, since "Videography" doesn't review software, they passed on the article. Still I think you'll find it to be a good overview of the possibilities of this medium.

I had to find out. It was long overdue. After all, it's been a year since I attended a CD-I conference. Just how far have CD-I's come since then?

I did participate in the last three big waves of video production: pay cable, home video, and infomercials. Am I missing a new bandwagon? Will people actually buy CD-I's and if so, why? Or, why not? What does the current crop of CD-I programs actually look like? In short–do they work? Is CD 4 me?

I decided that the best way to find out would be to spend a day looking at as many CD-I's as I could. A friend experienced with Philips' software who knows the best aspects of their CD-I's would be my guide, boosting me higher on the learning curve. I would evaluate what I saw as a <u>consumer</u> (*does it interest me?*), and as a <u>marketer</u> (*but how do you sell it?*), and, lastly, as a <u>producer</u> (*is there an opportunity here?*).

We used what looks like an ordinary CD player–a Philips CD-I player and a remote control device which you point at the screen and then a cursor appears. You can "click" the on-screen buttons to interact with the CD-I and get it to do things.

The flagship of the Philips CD-I collection is the impressive *Compton's Interactive Encyclopedia.* This monster disk has the 26 encyclopedia volumes condensed into 5200 articles which include slides and motion image clips, plus 32,000 short articles, and 130 picture montages with CD quality music and narration.

We started with a pathway called "title finder" and typed in–*"airplane"*–our subject. A text-filled screen appeared. (The articles are primarily text with some photos.) We clicked on the first photo in the article which started a narrated slide show of aviation history spanning from the early Wright Brothers' plane to the recent Stealth aircraft. Most clips run about a minute or less. Related articles–*fuselage, wings, engine mounts, landing gear*–also appear under "title finder."

In the encyclopedia, there are 19 subject areas–*art, earth, economics, geography, literature, religion, science, technology*, etc.–providing other pathways to access your area of interest.

Text scrolling was slow compared to my Macintosh computer. The text is very big and easy to read, but the page layouts lack inspiration. It really needs the touch of an art director or typographic designer.

CD-I's do not yet present acceptable full-frame motion video, so whatever video appeared was displayed in a frame about 1/6th of the screen size. This small video image is displayed in a graphic of an "entertainment room wall console" so that you feel like you are sitting in a room (the light dims) and watching television. Matting the small video into an environment is a clever way to get around the technical problem and takes the viewers' awareness off the fact they aren't seeing a full screen video picture. Nevertheless, the small frame video is not very involving. You are looking <u>at</u> something, rather than feeling like you are <u>in</u> the picture. For interactivity to really work, you have to feel like a part of it (e.g. virtual reality). CD-I's like *Escape from CyberCity* and *Lords of the Rising Sun* do an excellent job of involving the viewer in action. I am told that by the end of 1993 there will be full frame video.

There is a built-in *Webster's International Dictionary*. You can put your cursor on any word in the text, click on it, and a definition will appear. You can even click on words in the dictionary itself for definitions.

It's a shame that you can't print out your own reports (or download to your PC or Mac) from the CD-I player. This missing function hampers the CD-I players' usefulness.

There is also a world map. Click on your destination, and it zooms in. Click on the text for a country or city, and you get more articles, photos and facts. I got a little impatient. Compared to clicking around the channels on my television, this program feels slow. I want to scan the information at a much faster rate. However, I can easily imagine viewers–adults and children–wandering for hours through text and mini-videos learning and exploring at their own pace. I like it.

Philips was smart to feature this ambitious CD-I. It must have cost a bundle–millions?–to produce which will not be recouped through sales of the CD-I alone. Instead the program drives sales of the hardware. In one promotion, Philips offers a gift certificate for software: you have your choice of the encyclopedia (which retails for around $299) or several other lower priced CD-I titles.

Another personal favorite is *Gardening by Choice: Flowers and Foliage* in association with Ortho Books. (There is a second CD-I in production in association with *Better Home and Gardens* which provides much better name recognition for marketing.)

The basic menu is a United States map. You pick where you live, and the "climate zone" is instantly set. A house appears with six different types of flowers to choose from: *bulbs, perennials, house plants, container plants, annuals* and *roses*. Pick one. You are then asked to pick either "sunshine" or "shade," and you are shown a list of flowers which prefer sun or shade. You continue making selections such as *color* and *height*, and you end up with flowers that meet your specific criteria.

There are 600 index cards with descriptions of each flower: *name, type, light, height, space, when to plant, bloom, colors.* There is a personal "index box" where you can save the selection of your favorite flowers. There are also photos of every flower. Flowers are listed by both the common name and the botanical name.

There is a video demonstration on how to plant flowers in rows that is displayed on 6 panels within the full screen. This is another clever way to avert attention away from the smaller video image, and, in this case, it works very well.

Gardening is a terrific CD-I. It's very useful and engaging because you are customizing your own gardening needs. The potential of CD-I is clearly seen in this program.

Zombie Dinos From Planet Zeltoid ($39.98) is one of those games that sends dexterous users 12 years into pixel heaven. For the rest of us, well, it's a tough game to win. You travel back in time to locate and rescue dinosaurs before they are destroyed. It's a race against the Brain Blobs to save the planet. There are 14 scientifically accurate dinosaurs displayed in 3-D stop-motion. Very cool. There is live action footage (of dino character hosts) set in graphic environments. (Producers check these segments out!) This is a game designed to teach kids all about dinosaurs. Good choice of genres, Philips! Kids can't get enough of dinosaurs.

Beauty and the Beast: An Interactive Storybook Adventure ($19.98) has an interesting twist. Parents can set their child's age level at "*4 and younger*" or "*5 and older*." Parents can also turn audio prompts on and off; they can run the 28 minute show with or without subtitle story text. Besides the basic story, there are 75 "games" for each age level.

The beautifully produced, limited animation has rich effects, music and voice. The "games" teach recall, comprehension and creative thinking (they are really animated "multiple choice test questions." Here, I agree with the marketers–please, it's better to call them "games"). A voice responds to each choice. ("*Try again*").

135

The CD-I's slow interactivity works well with the kid's programming. Since the show's pacing is slow, you don't notice that the program is also slow. The technology matches the user's needs in this case.

More Dark Fables from Aesop, narrated by Danny Glover, is well written and uses quality limited animation. The CD-I has 12 stories. There are 36 puzzles based on each story. The morals of each story are explained, which is a nice programming touch.

Jazz Giants ($19.98) has 19 great classic legendary audio performances and a combination of slide show/paint box effects and text notes. The performances are outstanding and include the biggest names in jazz. (Great for the marketing marquee.) However, the title is ultimately disappointing, because there are <u>no</u> live action shots of the performers–only stills, many black and white. The quality of the surrounding graphics are poor, and this CD-I will certainly not age well. Well-written biographical and text notes are excellent and loaded with fascinating information on the recording session, the personnel, and music technique. But most buyers will only read this once. You have two choices: you can listen to the music alone, or listen with biographical notes.

What you are essentially buying is an audio CD packaged like a CD-I. The only reason a jazz aficionado would be buy the CD-I is that it doesn't cost any more than a CD and you get the linear notes. Buyers may feel burned here thinking they are getting something new. It's simply not sophisticated enough. Marketers know that when introducing new products–and especially something as important as a new line of AV programs–you have to keep the quality up or your customers won't be back for more. Bad choice here.

Rock Guitar ($69.98) gives you a choice of musical pieces that you can learn at your own pace. (We chose *Hendrix' Purple Haze*.) You can choose to <u>hear</u>: *lead, rhythm, lead and rhythm, lead and band*, or *metronome*, and you can choose to <u>see</u>: *lead, rhythm, or lead and rhythm* . You have great control over how you'd like to learn. You see the music score (each note illuminates when it is plucked–cool!), plus a small live action video picture of fingers playing the guitar. You can set the tempo, so that you can start slow and then move up to performing speed as you learn. The only place Philips missed here was that they should have included some name host (Eric Clapton?) to give the CD some marketing heat.

The Great Art Series: Art of the Czars ($39.98). Here you visit Russia's St. Petersburg and stroll through the city, stopping by the palaces and churches. You get a good feel for the city. Then you come to the Hermitage Museum, learn how it's laid out and where each school of painting (*Dutch Masters, Impressionists*) resides. You explore each collection and select the paintings you want to study. A voice over tells you the interesting features of your

136

selection. You can also view (pre-selected) close-ups of each painting. The reproduction of the paintings is only fair compared to the high resolution of an art book. The CD-I also includes the history of the tsars showing you what each built and what paintings each purchased for the collection. Fascinating stuff.

The high quality original music by Tchaikovsky, Grieg, Corelli and Rachmaninov is well placed for each painting school period.

Escape from CyberCity ($39.98) has full cel-animation and throws you into an action-packed movie as one of the characters. It's a shoot-em up where you try to infiltrate the city and escape. Very involving. Call in the 12 years olds with lots of arcade shoot-em-up experience or suffer a thousand grotesque deaths.

Lords of the Rising Sun ($39.98) is a fantasy samurai adventure set in 12th century Japan with armies, ninjas, swordsmen and archers. It combines the arcade-style "chop-em-up" ninja warriors with history, and war strategy as it utilizes actual Japanese castles and monastery locations. (Does the history and learning aspect help parents justify the purchase of what is essentially a violent program?) The graphics are terrific and make you feel you are there. A Japanese princess (live action video) in a fantasy graphic setting implores us to save her. Machos that we are, off to war we go. Moments later we are face to face with a ninja warrior who throws star-like weapons at us which progressively wounds us. We hear the realistic impact of the weapon cutting into our flesh and see our blood spatter against the shoji walls. Whoa! I'm dying! Awesome dude. No doubt this will be a big seller.

Producers should go to school on this one for the mix of live actors in pure graphic settings. The potential of computer blending of media and interactivity is just beginning.

The Best of Draw 50 is based on best selling books by Lee Ames. There are 50 illustrations that you can learn to draw one stroke at a time. Categories include: *monsters, vehicles, dinosaurs, buildings, athletes, animals, horses and Christmas.* We picked *Frankenstein* from the monster bin. You determine your own pace, erase or start over. You learn art tips along the way. There is a timer which lets you know how far into an illustration you are. Great for kids. Production is okay.

I've heard about, but haven't seen, what's touted to be the most popular new kids' CD-I, an "electronic coloring book." Kids pick characters and paint them, and the CD-I will play a cartoon utilizing the characters the kids have colored. (Is this a plot by the Harry paintbox manufacturer to train the next generation of video artists?)

Interactive Guide to the Colleges of Your Choice: The ACT College Search '92.
Your survey to over 3200 colleges. (I tried to find the best party schools, but
it doesn't have it.) This CD-I, however, has everything else you want to
know including student ethnic and religious mix. You can search for what
you want by certain curriculum criteria to narrow your choice down to 12
colleges. The CD-I them provides the addresses for the admissions office.

Summary

The jury is still out. It's too early to say whether this format will actually
make it. Sources tell me there are 20,000 CD-I players in the marketplace.
Prices are still high and exceed $1000 per player. Many CD-I's are co-
productions between PIMA (Philips Interactive Media of America) and
independent producers.

They've used some high profile promotable elements in the CD-I's, but
perhaps not as well as they could. They've probably spent as much as they
can on production, which is enormously expensive. However, those
consumers versed in higher quality film, video, graphics and print will find
that the production quality just isn't quite there.

I'm not ready to jump in until the installed base of buyers is much greater
because 1) if I go to all the trouble to produce a CD-I, I want a large
audience, and 2) the economics of production require it.

On the production side, what appears to be lacking most are skilled graphic
designers, typographers (where are the typographers!!), and art directors.
These are relatively inexpensive production elements that can bring added
value to the user's experience. Most of the CD-I's reviewed here are weak
on text design.

Philips is clearly trying to communicate that "CD-I's are for everyone," and
I feel they've made a very powerful opening statement with this round of
program offerings. Yet I still have the feeling that we are seeing the early
Model-T's coming off the assembly lines, and vast improvements will be
made in the months and years to come. We've got to start somewhere, and
it will take an enormous amount of energy and persistence (kudos to
Philips) on the part of the manufacturers, the marketers and the new media
producers to move CD-I's forward. I'm rooting for you all.

So, are CD-I's for me? Not yet. I'll sit on the sidelines for now. As for
producing, my strategy is to create proprietary properties that can be
translated into CD-I's when my time comes. So, on my next shoot, I'll bank
some extra footage for my first CD-I (or CD-ROM or...?)

Until then, go get 'em.

DIGITAL JAM SESSION

The premiere is at hand. At least 70 or 80 people are packed into one of the demo rooms at The American Film Institute (AFI) Apple Computer Center for Film and Videomakers in Hollywood. Two huge monitors stand at the front of the room. Between them are several laserdisc players, linked to a Mac Quadra 950 with 6MB of RAM, RasterOps' MoviePak, and various hard drives and other peripherals.

The Challenge

It all started early this year when Nick DeMartino, Director of the Center, called and asked if I'd participate in an upcoming two-day workshop at the AFI's Twelfth National Video Festival, February 4-7. The workshop was part of the Festival's Desktop Computer Media Division, a new event sponsored by this magazine and its quarterly supplement, *Videography's* QuickTime Professional.

Nick had invited half a dozen film-, video-, and other electronic moving-imagemakers to work together to create finished QuickTime "movies" in two days. On the third day this material would be transferred to laserdisc players and programmed. On the fourth, it would be premiered for the Interactive Media Salon, an ongoing evening event.

Step One: See Atchley's Performance

The first step was to see an interactive multimedia performance by video performance artist Dana Atchley. We would use his authoring system, which employs Macromedia's MacroMind Director (developed by Patrick Milligan, Atchley's collaborator and programmer). Atchley would guide us through the process, and at the end we'd have a collection of one and two-minute personal QuickTime stories to premiere on Atchley's interface.

The AFI's theater was packed; several hundred people had to be turned away. Atchley–a practitioner of the "Spalding Gray stage monologue tradition"–was inspiring. He squats down next to a monitor displaying a "video fireplace" and begins spinning stories. They are illustrated here and there with very short clips of artifacts, interviews, music, and text, which is projected on a large screen behind him. He interacts with these visual pieces and is able to stop or advance them with a remote control mouse. Atchley has prebuilt dozens of sequences. As his show starts, Atchley feels out the mood of the audience, selects some of the icons displayed on the large screen, and drags them down onto a "road" that is the linear path the performance will take. This way, the audience is aware of the structure of the performance–even if they don't know exactly what will be called up with each icon.

Dramatically this builds expectations and drama. Atchley tells a little story, moves around the stage, and confronts the audience. He selects an icon, and clicks on it; and something happens–often a video clip. He may let it play out while talking over it or singing along with it, or he may stop it and start it or skip it altogether.

It's his show, and he's not about to let the technology tell him what to do. That's the best part of what he's put together. He controls everything. His performance is not driven by the technology; rather he employs it, effortlessly, like a high-tech shaman.

Atchley has documented everything that ever happened to him on something like a dozen different visual formats. And at last, (Eureka!) along comes a technology that can finally put it all together! He can store it, access it, share it, and perform it.

Step Two: Decide What to Do

I was instantly inspired. Like many of us, I too have saved almost any visual element of my family's history. I wanted to put my life story into QuickTime as well. In 1974 I did that–sort of. After traveling for two years alone throughout Japan, Bali, India and East Africa, I made a one-hour autobiographical documentary called *Silver Box*. Then I toured art museums throughout the country, answering questions.

When I got to Seattle the local film reviewer bashed *Silver Box*. *"How could anyone be so egotistical to make a film about themselves?"* the reviewer asked. Excuse me, I thought. Painters, writers, sculptors and other artists use the material most readily available (themselves)–why can't filmmakers? But I didn't say that then. I was simply crushed, and never showed the film publicly again. Fast forward to the present, and I find myself inspired that Atchley was so courageous in using the material from his own life.

For me, it took several years to optically print everything (slides, photos, Super-8 and 16mm film) onto one medium: 16mm film. The collage effect actually worked quite well, as does Atchley's synthesis to the digital realm.

Our assignment for the workshop was to prepare a one or two minute piece–something we could complete in two days using QuickTime with PhotoShop and whatever else we could get our hands on. I have tons of material from various films and videos I've made (*Dolphin, Hardware Wars, Bucky Fuller, Diet For a New America*), that I could easily throw together. I'd have great images, high production values, and could make an impressive piece–but that was too easy. Atchley had challenged something in me, and I knew it was time to get back to my Silver Box idea. My piece would be very personal.

140

Other Influences On My Decision

I should also mentioned that I was equally motivated by a work that screened at the AFI following Atchley's performance. It was a QuickTime movie called *Big Warm Bear Arms*, by Greg Roach of Hyperbole in Houston, Texas. It had been named Best of Show just weeks earlier by MultiFacet Communications' Second QuickTime Festival, held during San Francisco's MacWorld Expo.

Roach, also the creator of the much-acclaimed *Madness of Roland*, had fashioned a QuickTime movie in which the images were hardly there: children running through a forest; special-effect fireflies; wonderful music and poetry by Roach. It was extremely evocative, and the audience was stunned into silence by its beauty.

What I loved about this piece was that he used QuickTime, with all its current funky-chunkiness; and it worked great. He didn't try to make it do something it couldn't. He used the inherent image quality to his advantage –something I've seen few others do. The images were almost shadows, and so the audience really had to participate and fill in. And to fill in they drew from their own childhood memories. And it really, really worked.

That's the kind of piece I wanted to make.

Step Two: Writing and Previsualization

First I looked at the emotional quality of my life over the last few years. I traveled to Bali; got married. We met a birth mother and father, and adopted a child. My mother died. Could I cover all of this in one or two minutes?

The night before the workshop I wrote a 45-minute script. Too long. Looking for the essence and evocative language, I ended up with one phrase and a few words for the graphics. The act of writing a long script got my creative juices flowing, and gave me a chance to review all the potential material I might use.

Step Three: Sharing Ideas

On the first day of the workshop, Atchley got the group of us talking about ourselves and what we thought we might want to do–digital therapy. It was a delicate matter.

I was looking for structure, so I'd know where my work would fit into the whole. But since the presentation was nonlinear, there is no beginning, middle, or end. Curiously enough, we each found we were working with

141

similar elements–weddings, Bali, adoption and fire. There was already some connection between what each of us was doing.

We all worked quietly on our own pieces. And from time to time, we'd help one another on a technique or a program. There wasn't much time. We had a show to put on!

Step Four: Finding Meaning in the Digitized Image

I digitized about 5 minutes of Hi-8 footage using Screenplay and Adobe Premiere. I started to cut a traditional kind of movie, but it wasn't looking right. As I worked with the postage-stamp size images, I realized that what I really was looking for were "open ended" icons and symbols that, to an audience, would be loaded with emotion and meaning. (Whether or not they got all the content that was there or that I intended was really a secondary issue.)

An underlying theme I worked with is the transitory nature of existence. Since I love Balinese shadow plays, I selected a single image–a "tree of life" leaf-like shadow puppet that fluttered like a huge moth against the flame from an oil lamp. It became my motif that opens the piece and at various times it acts as a transition. Even if you don't realize it's a shadow puppet, it feels magical, ritualistic, shamanic. I used it like it was some great paint brush passing over life events–changing, blessing, forming life itself.

It's tough to express all of this; it's clear how much more powerful images are than words. But paradoxically, it's only in the articulation of this that it seems clear what I was doing. Working with the images was an intuitive –almost unconscious–process, and I felt everyone was going through something similar. Experimenting, changing, trying again. With digital editing the changes are fast, the feedback immediate. With QuickTime, we are clearly dealing with an entirely new process. It's akin to video and film, but very different because it instantly combines so many elements and because the image quality is primitive and elemental.

Step Five: Editing

My shot list is rather short. The tree of life shadow puppet is my motif and transition element.

I tried to bring out the extraordinary in the ordinary, to find those transcendent moments in our lives that others would recognize, merge with, and make their own.

A very evocative cello solo bonded my images together. Occasionally, I would let an "ordinary reality" sound bleed through and then return to the transcendent world called forth by the music.

The tree of life and shaman at the beginning suggested mysticism, spirituality and ritual. From there I just played with the dynamics of the image and music and kept condensing the content in the images to just the essential. I did learn that the image has to be quite graphic to be easily read. I continued to boil my "alchemical pixels" down to a no-frills shot list:

> Bali Shaman reads Geraldine's palm
> *("You'll have two children...")*;
>
> MS silver wedding cup and our faces
> *("This cup represents union...")*;
>
> MS Geraldine at reception, in wedding dress
> *("I've waited a long time for this...")*;
>
> tree of life shadow puppet;
> silhouette of couple playing in surf;
> title: *birth parents*;
>
> birth mother's face smiling, wind blowing her hair;
>
> delivery room, man strokes pregnant women's head;
>
> doctor lifts newborn in air;
>
> newborn's fingers in my hand; portrait of baby;
>
> baby and Geraldine look into mirror
> *("What a pretty baby...")*;
>
> tree of life/cello diminuendo on audio track....

Impressions

I am very inspired by what you can do in QuickTime with Adobe Premiere. It's all there on one Mac screen: two video tracks, three audio tracks, a track for special effects (dissolves and wipes), and a graphics track. It's a poor man's Avid nonlinear editing system (which I have used). Digitizing is slow, previewing your piece is slow, and when it's time to have the computer "make your movie," you're better off going to lunch (my two-minute movie took about 12 minutes to process).

The Gear

Some of the hardware we used included a Kodak DCS 200 camera, several Sony and Canon Hi-8 cameras, SuperMac's Video Spigot, and a HP Scanjet Scanner. On the software side we used SoundEdit Pro, Adobe Premiere, Macromedia's MacroMind Director, Adobe Photoshop, Fractal's Painter, and Screenplay. Most of the computers were Quadra 700s or Mac IIci's. Harry Mott is the AFI's facilitator and assisted everyone in the workshop, but he still found time to create his own wonderful QuickTime movie on a Quadra 950.

Other Explorations

Most of my colleagues' pieces were very personal stories. Some were in the traditional documentary style. They worked fine. I think we need to explore what these QuickTime movies are really all about. Atchley and Roach certainly have their arms around it, and are doing the most innovative and free stuff I've seen yet.

The rest of what I've seen–not that much, really–consists of established media conventions and techniques wrapping. People are trying to do what they have done in other media, except now it's QuickTime. It's like the Burns and Allen television show from the early Fifties. Even though it was shot on film, they began and ended it with conventions that mimicked vaudeville and radio. A comedy skit was delivered on a stage complete with curtain and canned applause and laughter on the soundtrack. But Burns and the other early television pioneers figured it out. So can we. Let's allow the medium of QuickTime to show us what it wants us to do with it.

I'm convinced that those who take these new tools and use them like artists will find a whole new market for their work. New Age music grew out of a new tool (the synthesizer), and a new genre was created. If you create a killer QuickTime movie on CD-ROM, people will buy it.

Start working with this stuff. Take a class; read the quarterly *Videography's* QuickTime Professional. Go to a workshop, and buy a system. Get yourself on the learning curve and explore, and then teach others.

Step Six: Fame and Fortune

So there we were at the "Interactive Media Salon" premiere. Atchley showed some of his pieces. Then we each spoke briefly about the experience of the workshop and what we were trying to do. Then we showed our pieces.

I was nervous. I'd been working in video and film for the last 12 years, but have rarely been in the same room as my audience. Now my little movie was about to be shown to a packed room. Anticipation. My wife and daughter sat next to me, stars of QuickTime/my life. I hoped everyone would like it.

They did. The audience, which included all of the workshop participants, was fascinated, enthralled and even moved by our little movies. I sense that everyone had the feeling they were in on something–at the very beginning.

Now it's your turn. Go get 'em.

DESKTOP VIDEO: VISION AND APPLICATIONS

I couldn't resist adding this retro-article which is kind of a digital polaroid of the past. At the "Desktop Video" Conference, I first met editor Brian McKernan who asked me to write for "Videography" magazine. (This article did not appear, nor was it edited by McKernan.)

The event itself was the first I am aware of on the subject of desktop video. I pitched the "desktop video" conference concept to UCLA Extension (the sponsors). They didn't quite understand it, but were pleased when the auditorium was packed. The people who spoke continue to be luminaries of the new technologies.

Technically, the article is out of date, which shows just how very fast things are moving in digital video.

Desktop video! You've seen this catchword everywhere, but what does it really mean? A Desktop Video Conference sponsored by UCLA Extension tried to answer this question.

There were as many definitions of "desktop video" as there were speakers. Most agreed on these characteristics: 1) it's cheap and affordable; 2) it uses a computer platform; 3) it fits on a desk top; 4) video can be brought in and out from the platform; 5) it is multi-media and a hybridization of forms and formats; 6) it is an evolving and very fast changing format; 7) it is a coming together of film, video, television, graphics, text, animation, painting, storytelling, audio and music; 8) it's easy to use; and 9) it does everything you can do now with traditional video systems and gives you more control.

Sounds great to me. Where do you get one? Well, that's the crux of the problem. The vision is there, but there is no one, high quality integrated system. There is no one-stop solution for desktop video.

Once a low-cost, broadcast quality system comes into being, there will be a rush of creators from many disciplines scurrying into production. There were previous explosions of production in home music recording studios (thanks to MIDI-ed synthesizers) and in desktop published books, magazines and newsletters (thanks to the laser printer).

The conference was an information-packed day with participation from hardware and software companies, from video visionaries looking two to five years into the future, and from video producers who couldn't wait for the revolution to begin so they could put together their own desktop video systems. What follows is a kind of "frame grab" of the most interesting bits and bites.

147

"The boundaries begin to blur between media."

Eric Martin, former Dean of the School of Arts at the California Institute of the Arts, used a Macintosh to create images for a corporate presentation for IBM! Eric sees the congruence of all media coming into one digitized form. The producer's job is to somehow grab hold of this new and very powerful technology and to use it in ways that do not imitate earlier forms.

"Today's new format becomes tomorrow dim memory," cautioned Martin. "We have to struggle within us to become fluent and meaningful in our ability to manipulate these new tools and come up with new ideas." At the same time, there is a conservative bias to not see the meaning of what this evolving meta-medium is. Martin said, "All interesting new tools tend to first be used in the spirit of the tools they appear to replace." From what Martin has seen of many current paintbox operators, he thinks they must be asking themselves "how many highlights can dance on the head of a pin?" He said, "We can invent something subtle and powerful, but we don't know how to use it. We seem to have a genius for trivializing our tools–Porches get driven to supermarkets, Nikons get used for snapshots, and computers get used as glorified typewriters."

Reflecting back, he said, "Memory costs about 1/40th of what it cost in 1980. Ten years from now, a desktop computer will be 500 times more powerful than it is today. It's going to do different things. We have to realize that we're in just a moment, in a blur, and we're headed for something considerably more profound. Which is the ultimate digital collapse into a single box, into a single working environment, that's easy to use.

"This change is accelerating more at the desktop end when compared to the high-end. Desktop video is at the very start of a period of hybridization. We're really on the lip of an abyss. We're in for some profound changes. The computer is replacing all tools, because it increasingly is all tools. In the digital universe, a sound-is-a-tool-is-an-image-is-a-word-is-a-movement. Since it is all one language, the boundaries between media begin to blur. We're becoming one technology, one medium, and indeed, one decentralizing, interconnecting world culture. A lot of that is because of this technology."

"The new Hi-Band 8mm camera features a built-in time code."

The first piece in the desktop video puzzle begins with the camera, a primary tool for generating imagery. Conrad Coffield, Director of Marketing for SONY Professional Products, demonstrated several cameras and editing decks. The Sony EVO-9100 features high-resolution images of more than 400 TV lines. It uses two kinds of videocassettes, the Hi8ME (metal evaporated) and Hi8MP (metal powder) tape to deliver the high

148

quality image. Most important, the new Hi-Band 8mm camera features a built-in time code generator to record time code on the videocassette while it is recording images. This simplifies the editing process enormously. (No longer do you have to transfer 8mm to Beta, or 3/4", or 1" with time code in order to edit. Consequently, you do not lose one generation of picture quality as you previously did by bumping across to another editing format.) The 2 lb. camera also comes with a range of other accessories including rechargeable batteries, which makes it a unique low cost but high quality component to a desktop video system.

Nevertheless, SONY does market two new Hi8 recorder players. One is the EVO-9800. The other is a dual deck machine, the Video8 Video Memo Writer VCR, EVO-720, which includes two decks in a single housing with the ability to do quick edits, program edits, inserts and audio dubbing and some title recording. It comes with a jog dial and shuttle ring.

SONY's cameras are cheap and easy to use. However, Coffield made the point that the Hi-Band 8 was not designed to replace other existing SONY formats like Beta or 3/4". Each has its place. For example, the editing system is only accurate to a few frames.

Coffield was clear in pointing out that although many producers are looking to Hi-Band 8mm and producing some spectacular results, SONY does not as yet provide a complete Hi-Band 8mm production system as they do with the Beta format. Nevertheless, producers will undoubtedly experiment with Hi-Band 8mm, pushing the technical limitations as far as they can, and, in some cases, creating programs that are acceptable for broadcast.

Coffield spoke about work being done at SONY. "Clearly our future is an all-digital domain. 100 MB/sec really isn't enough to get the same kind of quality you get in analog. If memory was free, it would be no problem. So now analog is still the best compression format going for the professional market. We can't go backwards, we have to go forward. Digital is probably 4 or 5 years down the road that will offer the quality and performance this group will demand.

"New tools bring 'a new language' to the videomaker's repertoire."

An innovative device, which videomakers will flock to purchase for their Hi-Band 8 and S-VHS videocameras, is the Steadicam JR. Surprise guest, Jac Holzman, former chairman of Panavision and currently chairman of Cinema Products (which manufacturers the Steadicam JR) premiered this production tool to the public for the first time. He demonstrated how this new tool brings "a new language" to the videomaker's repertoire to eliminate bumps and jitters in hand-held camerawork.

149

Commodore Business Machines Graphics Marketing Manager Christopher Kohler demonstrated the AMIGA, a very low-cost integrated desktop video system. There are some limitations, such as resolution, which restrict it for many professional applications. It is being used in an "off-line" capacity, for example, in creating 3D frame models, which can then be further processed on other systems.

Combining video with graphics requires that the video image be loaded into the computer. Karen Mills demonstrated Mass Microsystem's new ColorSpace IIi board which is installed into a Macintosh II computer and allows for titles, graphics, animations and special effects to be laid over video. The video image can be digitized and combined with other images. Mass Microsystem's boards are used mostly for corporate television, business and institutional sales promotions, presentations and training.

> *"Two or three people still have to do the same work,*
> *which is possible with desktop video."*

John Rice, former editor of *Videography*, felt the first opportunities for desktop video are in the corporate market to be used for "sales and marketing, training, employee communications, in presentations, as internal memo communications, corporate public relations, motivation, special events and as video news releases."

Rice said, "There are videotape productions which cost $1000, and others which cost $1 million. Desktop video is bringing more people into video, and the computer is key. Where else do you have a large base of computer users than in corporate life? They are the first to see the applications. We are seeing a creativity of applications, all from the corporate market. As some corporations are reducing their video departments from 25 or 30 people to 2 or 3 people, they still have to do the same work–which is possible with desktop video."

Steve Sanz, David Watkinson and Scott Billups are creative producers, and each produces corporate videos, logos and commercials. Steve Sanz, showed examples of logos created, using Macromind Director, an animation program.

David Watkinson, who produced three 1-hour videos for a law firm, responded to audience concerns that much of the desktop animations they saw were "chunky." "Better broadcast stuff takes a lot of time to render, and the image you get on the screen can't refresh fast enough to be able to dump it out onto videotape in real time. So you have to send it out one frame at a time, which takes more time and effort. There is a whole market that doesn't care if things are chunky. And it's affordable for a whole new type of producer who before couldn't afford to do it. But with camcorders, they can shoot it, do animation and spice it up. They can do a 'Jane Fonda' workout tape or whatever they feel they are an expert in. And they can sell it mail order."

Watkinson talked about the competition. "With my Macintosh, I can almost compete with companies that have paintboxes for lower end industrials. Everything is 8 bit video dumped from a Macintosh real time. I use Macromind Director for animated titles. Macintosh and PC's hooked up to a laser disk is the platform of choice for interactive video, and that's coming on strong in education, in-house corporate training and kiosk presentations. In the interactive area, we are not trying to compete with the big guys, we are the big guys."

Scott Billups may have produced more desktop video hybrids than anyone. He gave us a walking tour through his "desktop video system." His system is configured for 3/4" U-Matic because "it's the standard format throughout the world. You can show it anywhere–agency, broadcast or cable. It doesn't have the best resolution; nor is it cost effective. But there are 2.5 million machines throughout the world. Hi-Band Pro 8mm is good for field gathering, but the tape doesn't stand up to editing."

Besides desktop video, Scott uses his system for scripting, storyboarding, budgeting and schedule breakdowns. "For industrials videos, I can make ancillary income because it is very easy to grab a frame off of a video, digitize it, and throw it into some desktop publishing software. The next thing you know, it's in your client's brochure."

"The Macintosh is sort of an all-terrain vehicle of computers."

Billups is waiting for engineers to design low cost desktop edit control systems. "In edit control, Macintosh is not going to be the leader. If you put it head to head with other equipment, it's going to lose miserably. Conversely, there is no other computer except the Macintosh that lends itself to all the various applications in desktop media. It's sort of an all-terrain vehicle of computers."

Billups's system consists of a video editing system, an audio sweetener and mixer, cinch generator, wave form editor, time base corrector and other more traditional pieces of equipment. He uses a Massmicro Color Space II ("which is very versatile") and Truvision's New Vista ("with 32 bit color, capable of very high resolution"). "For general industrial use, it's quite sufficient. But if you want to do something for broadcast, you'll want to use a real broadcast encoder/decoder. Purchasing one costs $6000, so you might want to rent it."

He uses a monitor that's capable of displaying both the computer non-interlace mode and the NTSC interlace mode. This gives him the capability of previewing graphics before they are laid down on video.

151

The programs he uses are MacroMind Director, LetraSet Color Studio (paintbox), Photo Shop, and Strata System–photo realistic rendering–all of which have similar applications to the high priced, professional Waveform or Personal Iris systems. He uses the Amiga as a pre-production tool. He says "the cost on Waveform for a short sequence will be $5000-10,000. On the Amiga, you can cut 60% off the budget. "

"The learning and investment curve is enormous in desktop video," said Billups. Scott recommended that "you go to seminars, manufacturers, and SIG's (special interest groups), and subscribe to *Mac Week*, *Videography* and *Film & Video Magazine* to keep up on the latest developments." His system costs between $180,000 and $250,000. Hardly "desktop" by our definition, but Billups's set-up successfully competes with systems costing 5 to 10 times as much.

"Audio is much further along than video."

Audio production requires less computer memory than video, which makes desktop audio production practical. Peter Gotcher, president of Digidesign, said, "Don't treat audio as an afterthought. Desktop audio systems can be operated by a non-technical person with a personal computer. Audio is much further along than video. You can do all elements of audio production with the exception of multi-track. Que-Sheet is our interface with video editing and creates editing lists for doing audio production.

Sound Tools is a professional system with 1300 systems installed worldwide. It costs $3200, and requires a Mac II (or SE) and a large hard disk. Sound Tools locks to time-code, and is a 2 channel, digital audio recording and processing system. It is software with a board that plugs into the Macintosh, which records CD quality sound to a standard Mac hard disk for editing and processing. Random access editing is 10 times faster, because you can immediately jump in real time between different audio elements. Gotcher said, "It's a lot more creative because you are willing to experiment. We're trying to put editing in the hands of creative people and remove the engineer or middleman which has been very time consuming and inhibiting to the creative process."

Audio Media is very similar and has all the audio circuitry on one Mac II card. It doesn't support time code but it will work with Macromind Director and Hypercard. This is designed for people who are working in a self-contained Macintosh environment with animation and hi-fidelity 16 bit sound and are not working with external image sources.

The choice between Sound Tools and Audio Media comes down to whether you are working with other image sources (like video which requires time-code) or just within the Mac.

Michael Backes is a visualization consultant to the Advanced Technology group at Apple and was a consultant on the special graphic effects for the film, *The Abyss*.

"The great thing about scanned art
is that it makes Rembrandts out of mental midgets."

"We called up our storyboards very quickly from a 160MB hard disk. We scanned them at 256 grey levels, which was 2 files of 75MB each. When they say multimedia eats hard disks, it's really true. I'm waiting for optical disks to mature because they will have 600MB on a cartridge and cost $50-100. Now I am using a drive from Mass Micro that holds 45MB on a removable hard disk cartridge that you can carry around.

"We used a Tectronics color printer with a grey scale ribbon to print out original copies of the storyboards to give to special effects for *The Abyss*. We used Pixel Paint, an 8-bit color paint program. We can take a storyboard and flip it, resize it, move it, and paint it. The great thing about scanned art is that it makes Rembrandts out of mental midgets."

Normally, in feature film production, you do drawings, painting and blueprints for the sets. Rarely does a director really know how the set will work until it's built. Backes has a novel computer solution. "On *The Abyss*, we drew a blueprint on a computer screen and had the computer turn it into a three dimensional drawing. We could use the mouse and literally walk around the set in real time. It was a wire-frame drawing without any major detail, but it did give you a sense of 3-D. The programmer is now doing a program called Walk-Thru that will be out later this year which will include light sources and shading. You can walk around the set and see if the camera will fit or whether the set will have to be enlarged."

When Apple introduced the Mac IIci in Los Angeles, John Sculley played a 4 minute animation in real time from a Mac on the screen. How'd they do that? Backes said, "It was coming directly off the hard disk. This was a technique called 'triple buffering' which is throwing three images from the disk up into the video RAM one at a time and doing a juggling act. It works great. We can get real time playback with 16 bit animation. The sound was played off a CD player, and we synced them. The computer had nothing to do with the sound."

There are also desktop solutions for creating commercials and on-air graphics said Backes. "Desktop video gives you the ability to capture video images from a videographics board like TruVisions Nu-Vista card (generates sync and is $7000), the Rastar Ops card ($1500), or the MassMicro card ($3000-4000). You can take a 3-D object and stick an animation on it. You can grab 15 seconds of *Casablanca* and mask it to a 3-D object, then move that object around and *Casablanca* plays back on it. It looks really great. Desktop video is expensive right now, because there are not a lot of one-board solutions. The Amiga is interesting, but I view it as a low-end solution. "

Al Alcorn is a member of Apple's Advanced Technology Group, and the inventor of Pong–the first interactive video game. He let us peek behind the doors at Apple.

> *"You will initiate the action in an artificial reality*
> *where the graphics will be fast enough*
> *to interact with human beings."*

Apple is busy working on "speaker recognition." Alcorn said, "The keyboard is not the best way to enter information–talking is the best way. We are building a software and hardware model on how the human ear works so the computer will recognize your voice."

Apple is also working with an animation-like in-betweening technology. Alcorn said, "We use constraint-based animation and modeling where we create an environment with laws of physics with mass, gravity and elasticity. You can deal with an object just like you would a real thing." He showed snippets of video research, such as an animation of a string which has no mass or gravity. Extending those principles to the 3-D world, he showed a Luxo desk lamp that had various base weights. The desk lamp was animated to jump. "We put in constraints, minimized muscle power, gave it a starting point and an end point. We made the Luxo lamp jump with various gravities, by just dialing up the base weight and making it heavier." The lamp leapt gracefully from one side of the frame to the other, until the weight was so heavy it seemed hard pressed to move only a few inches. The gravity built into the program gave an extraordinarily realistic look to the movement, which was done without conventional animation in-betweening.

Alcorn gave us a sense of an interactive media in an artificial reality space. He said, "Instead of someone scripting the action, you will initiate the action in an artificial reality where the graphics will be fast enough to interact with human beings."

Jim Fancher is a producer and system designer at Pacific Ocean Post. Having worked with most of the new technologies, he was able to give an overview on what's missing in desktop video.

> *"This year what we'll see is a 3rd wave of video boards*

with a compression algorithm working at real time video rates."

"There are two types of editing systems. Linear editing plays back tapes in sequence. Non-linear creates a huge data base from which you can random access your material. No more tape searching. The non-linear system creates a play list where you create pointers to information, and when you ask it to play it back it sequences it back out. There are a number of professional non-linear editing systems, Montage, EditDroid and a few others. All have found niches in video post production. Most are very expensive and aren't desktop video.

"In desktop video, there is the AVID, which uses non-linear editing, and a linear editing system from Larry Seehorn. There is also a HyperCard editing system that has not been released, and another from Julian Systems. All are geared to 1/2" or 3/4" tape for analog acquisition and editing. Except for AVID, they all emulate linear editing systems. AVID costs $80,000, if you want it to work.

"I haven't seen any Mac-based editing systems that I would want to live with. There are many editors in IBM that do a good job of machine control working through the VLAND type of interface. ASC, CASE System, is $7000 including the computer. It won't do graphics. The IBM PC is a very cheap solution as a platform for linear editing."

In addressing the "chunky" graphics question, Fancher said, "The issue is software. So far on Mac we haven't seen good software. The reason that the animation you see is so chunky is because it's calculated on a frame basis. Even where you get Macromind Director to move a circle, it still looks chunky because it is frame-by-frame at 30 frames per second. Higher end systems are all doing it at 60 fields per second.

"Mac just can't display 30 frame video, so when you get very complicated objects in Macromind Director it slows down. You might get 2 or 3 frames per second updated on the Mac, which isn't fast enough. So the only solution to that is to put things out non-real time, just like I do it in a 3-D graphics program–a frame at a time."

Fancher's work at Pacific Ocean Post has taken him into the digital desktop video realm. He said, "We're getting out pictures in the digital domain. D1 is an agreed upon, international standard for digital television and is the closest to a computer type picture. The bus speed just isn't there to get pictures out of the Macintosh in real time. For example, moving 25 MB/sec fills up your 40 meg hard disk in 2 seconds. We were looking for something that would store a whole lot of data, and we came up with 8mm tape. We work with a company that manufactures a tape drive that utilizes the same tape transport that goes into the Hi8 machines. They modify that tape transport into a data stream to back up systems, which allows you to record data on the tape. So we're not doing an analog recording on the tape, we are doing digital recording which holds 2.2 gigabits of information and gives us the storage capacity for digital television. The drives run about $5000. I can store about 50 seconds of real time broadcast television on a tape. The bad news is that it takes 2 hours to get it on video, off frame by frame."

Fancher creates full broadcast quality 3-D animations on the Swivel 3-D program and puts them out onto 8mm tape. "It's $5000 and is the equivalent of a $140,000 broadcast recorder. It takes 20 seconds a frame to output it to an 8mm tape."

Fancher sees data storage as the main problem now. However, image compression becomes one solution. "The walls we were up against with recording real time motion pictures on the Macintosh were bus speeds and data storage. At several megabytes per picture or 25 MB/sec of data, storage would rapidly exceed data storage. But if you begin to get significant amounts of compression, you can store significant amounts of pictures on standard hard disks. Compression programs like Stuffit give you a 2:1 compression. You can compress 6 megs to 3 megs. This year what we'll see is a 3rd wave of video boards with a compression algorithm working at real time video rates which will let you to store broadcast quality images on reasonably sized hard disks hooked to your computer."

Michael Nesmith was one of the first music video pioneers. He was the first to start a videotape distribution company (Pacific Arts Video) over a decade ago, and he was the first to publish a videomagazine. His eloquent luncheon speech gave the conference attendees a lot to chew on.

> *"This ability has uncovered another world–*
> *another place that only exists*
> *in the world of the computer."*

"As computers made their evolutionary journey, they went from huge clunky machines standing alone barely reachable by man to small portable devices that could communicate with each other. This ability to communicate was a powerful and under-appreciated force in the life of a computer. This ability has uncovered another world, another place that only exists in the world of the computer. Even though this world has no fixed boundaries, it is very, very real. It is cyberspace. It is the world of <u>virtual reality</u>. It has an incredible importance to you, and me, and the world as we know it.

"Everything you've been hearing about in today's conference is coming together to give us a look at this new virtual world. We have in our hands the tools to discover more and more of the virtual world and to define it in some degree. The computer has helped us discover a new world, and now we have a window through which we can look at it. We don't have to sit typing into the computer to retrieve the ideas. With desktop video, we can see it.

"We've got a lot of growing to do. The language of film, which has been created for a two-dimensional, single point-of-view, now has to expand to include the multi-dimensional multi point-of-view. The present techniques of filmmaking now become just a point of departure rather than a mature skill. The power of the video camera, coupled with the computer and the power it has to see the virtual world, gives us a new opportunity to define this world and make it beautiful just for beauty's sake."

While the vision of desktop video hasn't perhaps been invented yet, there are numerous indications that companies and producers are working fast and furious to bring it into reality. It will be at least another year before we see desktop publishing systems that will allow producers to take in analog video, digitize it, store it their computers, use non-linear, random access systems to edit sound and picture, and then lay the images out of the computer onto high quality tape. If we can't do all of it today (at personally affordable prices), we can certainly do pieces of it. The conference indicated to many that there's every reason to start experimenting now with some of the tools that exist for your current projects.

Now tool up, and go get 'em.

AVAILABLE FROM MICHAEL WIESE PRODUCTIONS

PRODUCER TO PRODUCER
The Best of Michael Wiese from VIDEOGRAPHY Magazine

by Michael Wiese

Edited by Brian McKernan,
Editor, VIDEOGRAPHY

Current information
about producing,
financing, marketing
and creativity is vital
to the videomaker.
Michael Wiese's
"Producer to
Producer" column in
VIDEOGRAPHY
magazine has
provided independent
producers with
cutting-edge insights
on the business of
video: program
development,
production,
financing, marketing
and distribution.

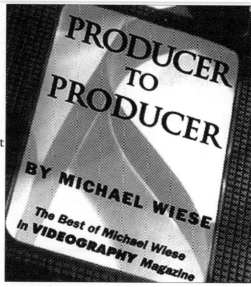

In an informal and
entertaining style,
Mr. Wiese draws on his own experience and that of other successful
video producers to demonstrate forward-thinking industry
practices.

Includes: "Shaking the Money Tree," "Zen and the Art of the
Steadicam, Jr.," "Where Do you Get the Money?," "Infomercials:
Where's the Info?," "Self-Distribution," "You Can Make Desktop
Video–But Can You Sell It?" and much more.

176 pp., illustrations
$19.95, ISBN: 0-941188-15-9

Film Directing
SHOT BY SHOT
by Steven D. Katz

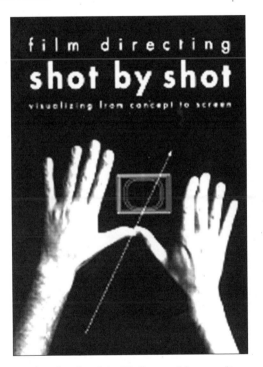

The most sought after book in Hollywood by top directors is filled with visual techniques for filmmakers and screenwriters to expand their stylistic knowledge. Includes storyboards from Spielberg, Welles and Hitchcock.

$24.95, 376 pp., 7 x 10
750 illustrations and photos ISBN 0-941188-10-8

FILM & VIDEO FINANCING

by Michael Wiese

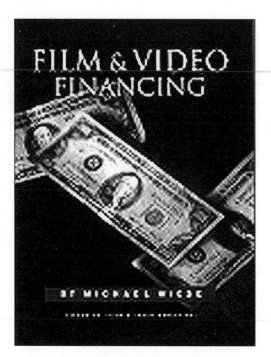

Praised as a book that prepares producers to get the money! A "palette" of creative strategies for producers in financing their feature films and video projects. Interviews with the producers of "sex, lies & videotape," "Trip to Bountiful," and "T2."

$22.95, 300 pp., ISBN 0-941188-11-6

Film Directing
CINEMATIC MOTION
A Workshop for Staging Scenes

by Steven D. Katz

The long-awaited sequel to Katz's best-seller —*SHOT BY SHOT*. A staging and blocking guide with 24 basic variations covering many dialogue and dramatic situations.

Includes interviews with John Sayles, Van Ling, Dusty Smith, Ralph Singleton, Allan Daviau, and Harold Michelson.

$24.95, 7 x 10, 320 pp., 200 illus., ISBN 0-941188-14-0

THE WRITER'S JOURNEY
Mythic Structure for Storytellers & Screenwriters

by Christopher Vogler

An insider's look at how master storytellers from Lucas to Spielberg have used mythic structure to create powerful stories which tap into the mythological core which exists in us all.

Writers will discover step-by-step guidelines and learn how to structure plots and create realistic characters. A Hollywood studio head made the rough draft for this book required reading for his entire executive staff.

$22.95, 283 pp.
ISBN 0-941188-13-2

INDEPENDENT FILM & VIDEOMAKERS GUIDE

by Michael Wiese

A classic best-seller and an independent producer's best friend. Advice on limited partnerships, writing a prospectus, market research, negotiating, film markets, pay TV and home video buyers.

$18.95, 392 pp., 45 illustrations, ISBN 0-941188-03-5

FILM & VIDEO MARKETING
by Michael Wiese

Secrets of marketing you can use today! This insiders' book shares industry marketing techniques you can use with investors, exhibitors, audiences, distributors, home video suppliers, wholesalers and retailers. You can't afford *not* to read this book.

$18.95, 512 pp., 77 illus., ISBN 0-941188-05-1

FILM & VIDEO BUDGETS

by Michael Wiese

A simple "how-to" budget guide for many types of films and videos. Clearly written, informal in style, the only book of its kind. Readers can look up sample budgets similar to their own and find a wealth of savings. A perennial best-seller.

$18.95, 348 pp., 18 budgets, ISBN 0-941188-02-7

MW

MICHAEL WIESE PRODUCTIONS
4354 LAUREL CANYON BLVD., SUITE 234
STUDIO CITY, CA 91604
818.379-8799•FAX 818.986-3408

**$** **=**

HOME VIDEO:
PRODUCING
FOR THE
HOME MARKET

↓

SEND MY
FREE
BOOK

"HOME VIDEO:
PRODUCING FOR THE
HOME MARKET"

I HAVE ORDERED **3**
ITEMS OR MORE.

Credit Card Orders
Call
1-800-379-8808
or Fax Your Order
818-968-3408

SUBTOTAL

SHIPPING (SEE CHART)

8.25% SALES TAX (CALIFORNIA ONLY)

TOTAL ENCLOSED

PLEASE MAKE CHECK OR MONEY ORDER PAYABLE TO _MICHAEL WIESE PRODUCTIONS._

SHIPPING

1 ITEM	$3.50
2 ITEMS	5.50
3 ITEMS	6.00

FOR EACH ADDTL. ITEM ADD 1.00

(FOR EXAMPLE, SIX ITEMS = $9.00)

FOREIGN ORDERS
MUST BE PREPAID

EACH BOOK SURFACE MAIL $4
EACH BOOK AIR MAIL $7

PLEASE ALLOW 2-3 WEEKS FOR DELIVERY.

ALL PRICES SUBJECT TO CHANGE WITHOUT NOTICE.

CREDIT CARD: _____ MASTER CARD _____ VISA (CHECK ONE)

COMPANY P. O. # _____

CREDIT CARD NUMBER _____

EXPIRATION DATE _____

CARDHOLDER'S NAME _____

CARDHOLDER'S SIGNATURE _____

NAME _____

ADDRESS _____

CITY _____ STATE _____ ZIP _____

TELEPHONE _____